LOVE IS AT THE ROOT OF RESISTANCE

STRATEGIES of ACTIVISM, ADVOCACY, and LIBERATION

GYASMINE GEORGE-WILLIAMS, Ph.D.

7 TEN

Legacy

LLC

◇◇◇◇◇◇◇◇◇◇◇◇◇◇◇◇◇◇◇◇◇◇◇◇◇

For my mother, Gerri George
The first Black woman I ever loved with all of my heart.
May your love shine through my soul as I live without you.

For my father, Clarence George
May your fire fiercely light my path in the darkness
as I move forward, honoring your memory.

To my ancestors
You outnumber my fears. I will forever feel your power.

To my son, Austin
May you feel my undying heart, protection, and love in every fiber of your being.
I hope I make you proud. Thank you for choosing me as your mother.
I will love you until my dying day and forever more.

To Aaron
Zora Neale Hurston proclaims there are
years that ask questions and years that answer.
Husband, our journey together has been filled with both.
I thank you for your love ,which has nurtured me to flourish as a woman,
wife, mother, friend, activist, and scholar. Until the wheels fall off.

◇◇◇◇◇◇◇◇◇◇◇◇◇◇◇◇◇◇◇◇◇◇◇◇◇

7 T E N

Legacy

LLC

7 Ten Legacy, LLC
Ontario, CA 91761

Publisher: 7 Ten Legacy, LLC
Interior Design and Editing: Linda Wolf, Network Publishing Partners, Inc.
Cover Design: Joshua Swodeck, Swodeck, Inc.
Cover Photo: Clay Banks on Unsplash
Author Photo: Christine Guzman, LCSW

Printed in the United States of America
First Edition: March 2021

ISBN Paperback: 978-0-578-86466-2

Library of Congress Control Number: 2021903618

TABLE OF CONTENTS

FOREWORD

Some may call her Gyasmine, Dr. G, Dr. George-Williams, sister, niece, friend, cousin, or mom, but I have the privilege of calling her my wife. I write this foreword as a proud husband and the father of our son. I've had the pleasure of supporting a brilliant and beautiful Black woman on her journey in activism and, as I look back over the years, I have seen a fire burning inside her as her passion for activism grew to advocate for marginalized people. This fire started with a flicker and has grown into a fierce blaze that is taking the world by storm. When we were dating, I remember having deep conversations about her parents, who are no longer with us, and how they were down for the cause, confirming that activism is in her DNA. She stands on the shoulders of two parents who taught her to fight the power of the oppressor.

Although some may call this movement a fad for the moment, living her activism is something that Dr. George-Williams was born to do. I have witnessed firsthand the journey of her birthing the concept of the book and watching her write while pregnant with our son. And shortly after giving birth, doing edits while rocking him to sleep is an example of her love, hard work, and dedication to helping others discover how to walk in their activism. Watching her during this process was truly magical and inspiring. She is a perfect example that anything is possible with faith in God and commitment to the people. The fire that is burning inside of her cannot be extinguished; it burns so vigorously because her calling is to ignite their voices to fight systems of oppression.

This book is a labor of love and, as her husband, I can truly testify to that. I am so proud of her. Dr. Gyasmine is a powerful, passionate Black woman who has found a way to help people, companies, athletes, and organizations seek advocacy and liberation. I cannot wait to see what God has next for her.

With love and solidarity,
Aaron Paul Williams, M.S., M.Ed., PPS

INTRODUCTION

*There comes a divine collision of your purpose and passion,
and that will provide your platform.*

Take a knee. March for all Black lives. Utilize your voice. Recognize and leverage your privilege to speak truth to power. These and so many more are all necessary actions of activism in the face of the racism and discrimination that has plagued Black, Indigenous, and People of Color (BIPOC), and disenfranchised groups for decades. As a Black woman, activist, researcher, former athlete, and coach navigating life with a Black former athlete husband, Black brothers, sisters, nieces, nephews, and friends of color as well as of indigenous groups, this work is deeply personal. The time is now.

My growth and journey as an activist is why this handbook is so important and so special to me. First let's start with my DNA—my mom, and my dad. Because of them, I am the perfect blend of an educator and an activist. My mother was an educator in the Los Angeles Unified School District for 37 years. Her form of activism was cloaked in love and liberation through arts and education, while leading strikes in between raising three beautiful Black children. And in his younger days, my father was a member of the Black Panther Party for Self-Defense.

I can remember as a child cleaning out our garage in the house I grew up in after my father passed away. Looking through my father's old boxes, I welcomed the likes of the *Autobiography of Malcolm X*, works by James Baldwin, records by James Brown (*Say It Loud: I'm Black and I'm Proud*), and "To Be Young, Gifted, and Black" by Nina Simone, just to name a few. And my favorite book was *Look Out, Whitey! Black Power's Gon' Get Your Mama!* by Julius Lester. Yes, that is an actual book. I wanted to know more about the contents of those boxes and, more important, the contents of my father's life, which began the journey of exploration of my activist DNA and destiny.

I was born and raised in an area of Southern California where my surroundings were extremely diverse, somewhat of an "It's a Small World" Disneyland atmosphere. I received backhanded compliments of being "so cool for a Black girl," or people saying, "You speak so well and you're so articulate." Friends often wanted to touch my hair. Yes, they tried to touch my hair. I frequently found myself serving as an informal representative for all Black people, and Black women in particular, in a multitude of spaces in my personal, educational, and professional life.

Those moments never sat right with me, yet in my naivety, I felt myself drowning in microaggressions and covert racism. I lacked the tools and vocabulary to challenge those moments without my anger and frustration overshadowing those situations with my white counterparts. I was alone in my resistance and the constant challenge of white supremacy and privilege, so I entered a space of retreat with a great deal of dissonance, searching for a place to safely share all of my complex layers and build my voice.

The feeling of onlyness was a repeat offender in my upbringing and still occurs. This not only occurred in my world, but also in my family, as I am like no one. I'm boisterous, tenacious, confident, and unapologetic in all of my identities. My twenties were a very special time in my Afrocentric identity development. I was a frequent performer at open mic nights, reciting spoken word poetry with my Members Only jacket and Mercedes-Benz medallion, while NWA (Niggaz Wit Attitudes), Public Enemy, and Queen Latifah were in heavy rotation in my musical rolodex.

I was so unapologetically Black and proud. And because of that I have been called the "angry Black woman." In some circles, I've affectionately earned the nickname Baby Huey, referencing Huey P. Newton, one of the founders of the Black Panther Party for Self-Defense, because I am the one who initiates uncomfortable yet necessary conversations that push the envelope and defy conventional modes of communication. These are conversations that I would have eagerly held with my belated father, and I know we would have had a good time. I began to realize I shared the physical features of my mother, but the inner workings of my father, and I strived to continue my family's legacy.

Yet, as the years passed, I was exhausted.

As I continued to grow in my academic and professional career, I became increasingly aware that institutions and systems belonged to and operated in a space of critical race theory's tenet known as interest convergence theory. Interest convergence is based on the premise that BIPOC's interest in achieving racial equality advances only when those interests "converge" with the interests of those in power. At previous institutions, I was asked to serve on countless diversity committees and to back numerous initiatives. My body was at the table, but my voice wasn't. Pictures of me were plastered on the homepage of the college's website multiple times. The university could now check its diversity box—after all, there's a Black woman on the homepage.

At the turn of the 21st century, society witnessed Black citizens losing their lives at the hands of the police and neighborhood vigilantes, which gained media attention. The February 26, 2012, murder of Trayvon Martin by civilian and neighborhood vigilante George Zimmerman and the nonsanction of his murderer fueled the social movement known as Black Lives Matter. Some activists and scholars have called his death, and many other deaths, public executions by law enforcement.

The deaths of unarmed Black men, boys, and women were both shocking and heartbreakingly predictable, because this is not a new phenomenon. Furthermore, the nonsanctioning of police officers operationalizes the disregard for Black lives. The disturbing trend of the fight against this disregard is the bedrock of the Black Lives Matter movement, which was born from the outrage of a generation that chose to stand up for justice to dismantle oppression.[1]

I recall the week before I attended my orientation for my doctoral program, Sandra Bland mysteriously lost her life after being detained in a jail cell overnight in Waller County, Texas. Her death had a deep and profound impact on my life, as she too was a higher education professional who was passionate about social justice and equity. I saw myself in her, and her death shook me to my core. I did not want to take this privilege of earning my Ph.D. lightly in the wake of the reemergence of activism in times of racial and social injustice. As a Black woman in higher education, I wondered, what could I do to evoke change and speak truth to power?

My education, activism, and former identity as an athlete are my foundation. Built on that foundation, my bias as a Black, cisgender woman who has experienced systemic racism in multiple forms shapes my research and practitioner lens. As I continue to gain knowledge about the untold history of this nation, centuries of perpetual and systemic racism oppressing people of color and disenfranchised groups, my consciousness deepens, and I see the world through a much more critical lens.

These experiences have shaped my belief that without education, activism is null. Educating myself on issues in which one is fueled is imperative to truly make a difference. I continue to engage in multiple forms of activism through research, education, scholarship, protests, and community building. Those moments began my journey into honoring a piece of me that I will never take for granted. This handbook is one of those actualizations of my activism.

Who Should Read This Handbook

This handbook will serve a multitude of individuals. Some are reading this with the awareness of injustices but have had a level of privilege where they didn't have to engage in activism or advocacy, or they may have engaged periodically when their comfort level served them. Some are reading this who are also aware of some injustices, but may have felt too overwhelmed to engage, felt directionless, or were plagued with white fragility or white guilt. And because of that, they have said and done nothing to utilize their voices for the voiceless or even for themselves.

However, there is a large group of readers who are truly unaware of injustices, or at least not aware of how heinous the climate of America still is. They are unaware of the stain of white supremacy that continues to infiltrate all spaces in this nation and in this world and shielded with a veil of protection that their privilege bestows upon them. This unique time and space in our world, with the COVID-19 pandemic and the stoppage of the hustle and bustle of life with mandatory stay-at-home orders, has offered a crash of consciousness and quarantine, bringing a flood of reality and birthing rage, guilt, sadness, and all the emotions in between. The reality of watching a cop place his knee on the neck of George Floyd for eight minutes and forty-six seconds as the world watched him beg for his life, exclaiming that he could not breathe as he called out for his late mother, has compelled people to move, to act, to speak up, and to use their voices for the voiceless.

And last, there are self-identifying activists and advocates who are reading this handbook who have engaged in forms of activism but are simply exhausted. This work is truly tiring, and they are exhausted from racial battle fatigue, caregiver fatigue, and race-based trauma through their fight for social justice. They are looking for strategies to engage and empower themselves and others.

Wherever you are on the spectrum of speaking truth to power, you are welcome. This handbook is for you. Whether you are a student, early-career professional, coach, school administrator, parent, caregiver, mentor, or member of a marginalized community, or you identify as an ally or accomplice, Audrey Geraldine Lorde says "Without community, there is no liberation".[2] So let's get liberated.

Similar to the impetus of the birth of Black Lives Matter, this handbook is born from a place of grief and pain from witnessing the modern-day lynching and injustices of fellow brothers and sisters at the hands of police and neighborhood vigilantes. In order for this handbook to be rooted in truth and power, it must be rooted in the experiences of not just my own journey of activism, but in the narratives of BIPOC and other disenfranchised groups.

Documenting and gaining understanding of their stories and journeys toward social justice advocacy through their activism is a critical part of centering this work and is necessary for a multitude of reasons. Scholars and practitioners believe doing this confirms that (a) reality is socially constructed, (b) stories are a powerful means for destroying and changing mindsets, (c) stories have a community-building function, and (d) stories provide mental self-preservation to members of outgroups.

This handbook was built from years of research, experience, and studies I have conducted capturing narratives of minoritized, marginalized, and oppressed students, athletes, practitioners, and members of the community who have shared their hearts, minds, and souls with me. And for that, I am forever grateful. As the stories of BIPOC and disenfranchised groups continue to be centered in research and literature and particularly this work, education and society will have no choice but to change its landscape. May this handbook be a road map through that tapestry of change.

As I've said, this handbook is deeply personal. I hope you feel my passion and love, as well as my lifelong fight and duty to serve others and fight for justice, in this work.

How the Handbook Is Laid Out

It is my hope that everyone will read both Part One and Part Two, as the two parts of this handbook are designed to be complementary. Part One is focused on the unique challenges faced by college athletes, college students, and community activists from Black and marginalized communities. This section provides a road map for the growth, development, and actualization of their activist identity as well as a source for empowerment. Part Two provides guidance to those who wish to support these athletes by growing in their own roles as allies and accomplices.

Coupled with research and narratives of the experiences of students, athletes, practitioners, and community members as they relate to activism, the Activism Growth Model™ (AGM) is introduced in Part One as a set of sequential steps for all who desire to do the inner work in order to make a difference in their personal lives as well as in the spheres of influence around them and beyond.

Prior to the creation of the AGM, my dissertation capturing the lived experiences of Black College Athlete Activists (BCAAs) was birthed, as it was truly a labor of love. Because I had the honor of serving and working with this unique student population, Part Two of the book will introduce another guide known as the Black Athlete Activist Leadership Model™ (BA²L) that I created for those who work with BCAAs, Black student activists, and activists of color as a framework to engage, understand, educate, and support the growth of these groups.

Both Part One and Part Two were written to enlighten and empower all who stand at the front lines of this battle against inequity and injustice—those who have inherited inequity and injustice, as well as all who wish to end it.

May this handbook be a lighthouse for you in a time where you may feel directionless in your journey to use your voice. May my blood, sweat, and tears become a testimony and serve as fuel to find, sharpen, and live fully in your calling toward activism and advocacy.

In solidarity,

Dr. G

PART ONE

For Activists, Present and Future

◇◇◇◇◇◇◇◇◇◇◇◇◇◇◇◇◇◇◇◇◇◇◇◇

CHAPTER ONE

History and Background of College Activism

Laying the Foundation: Identifying Anti-Blackness and Defining Racism and Activism

In order to truly engage in activism and resistance toward oppression, racism, and white supremacy, it's imperative to understand the concept of anti-Blackness as it permeates every facet of society. Anti-Blackness epitomizes the resistance to acknowledge the Black individual as human and worthy of equality. This has been demonstrated through historical evidence of deeply embedded anti-Black institutional policies and practices.[3] Mills[4] argued that anti-Blackness is the driving tool of the *social contract*, which he defined as the societal arrangement that whites are human, and nonwhites are not and should not receive the simple civil rights belonging to human beings.

For the purpose of this book, the terms *Black* and *African American* will be incorporated simultaneously throughout. I will do this because some believe the term *African American* is too limiting and prefer to use the term *Black* to encompass the diaspora of this very beautiful population. Anti-Blackness in the social contract was blatantly demonstrated in one of the most adverse and overt examples of anti-Blackness in history known as the three-fifths rule. This was a legally binding document established in 1787 stating African Americans were only three-fifths of a human being and deserved the liberties and freedoms of nothing more than an animal.[5] Consequently, anti-Blackness continues to drive the policies, procedures, and perceptions that harm the progress of Blacks and African Americans in the current racial climate of the United States.[6]

The resurrection of activism today is motivated by the continuous murder of Black boys, men, and women at the hands of police where officers receive no sanctions—a modern-day lynching. The term "lynching" will be used this way throughout this handbook. This type of behavior is a clear illustration that racism is alive and causing pernicious harm to the bodies and minds of Black people and all those who fall under the hierarchy of the social contract.

Defining Racism

Racism is the belief and physical actions of superiority of one race over another, which results in blatant or disguised discrimination and prejudice toward people based on their race or ethnicity. Racism, as defined by Solorzano, Allen, and Carroll,[7] exists when one group believes itself to be superior and has the power to demonstrate racist behavior. Taylor and Clark[8] described racism as a normal component of daily life for Black people and people of color. Harper[9] defined racism as:

> "*individual actions (both intentional and unconscious) that engender marginalization and inflict varying degrees of harm on minoritized persons; structures that determine and cyclically remanufacture racial inequity; and institutional norms that sustain white privilege and permit the ongoing subordination of minoritized persons.*"

Racism is an endemic and permanent aspect of the experiences for people of color that has and will affect every facet of their lives. It has become pervasive, constant, and engrained in established structures, but dominant populations often ignore, do not recognize, or do not acknowledge racism's reality.[10] Racism is not a random, isolated act, and structural influences such as institutional racism, discrimination, and status work together to influence the behaviors and experiences of Black people and people of color.

As a qualitative researcher for many years, I have witnessed the prevalence of racism, and the participants' lived experiences and counternarratives in my research and work confirmed this prevalence, forming the cornerstones of how this handbook was constructed. Identifying racism informed my understanding of the experiences of the participants, their journey toward anti-racism engagement, and the strategies they used in their growth and advocacy. My goal is that this handbook will serve as a guide for your journey.

Diversity in Racism

Yes, there is diversity in racism. What do I mean by that? Simply that there are different types of racism that operate and have operated successfully throughout history. In order to be a part of the community to dismantle racism, you must identify all the ways in which it has permeated all systems.

Institutional Racism

Cromer and Millan[11] define institutional racism as policies and practices within and across institutions that produce outcomes that chronically put a racial group at a disadvantage by the distribution of resources, power, and opportunity to the benefit of people who are white and to the exclusion of people of color. This has manifested in systems such as education, healthcare, housing, the criminal justice system, and employment, just to name a few, but historically in all facets of society.

Can you think of instances in which policies and procedures in one or many of these systems have structurally benefited or maintained a space of superiority over Black, Indigenous, and People of Color (BIPOC)?

_____

_____

_____

_____

Systemic/Structural Racism

Systemic or structural racism is a set of social, economic, and political systems where public policies, institutional practices, cultural representations, and other norms work together in ways that reinforce and perpetuate racial inequality.[12] Systemic racism exists because systems of oppression work as they have been historically meant to. The most visceral illustration of this was the institution and system of slavery that had no intention of ever ending after the transatlantic slave trade ended, because slavery did not end then. Generations of enslaved people were born into slavery in the United States. Systemic or structural racism enables institutional racism and that is how it permeates all systems.

Interpersonal Racism

Interpersonal racism is acts of racism between individuals that are birthed from biases created by the racism framework of the system that translates to the interactions that one has with other people.[13] We've seen interpersonal racism displayed countless times as "Karens" and the like take it upon themselves to call the police on Black individuals for existing, knowing that once law enforcement is involved with a Black person, death or physical harm may ensue.

These diverse avenues in which racism is displayed can be in overt, blatant, or covert ways that may be more difficult to identify immediately. Nonetheless, as an activist and advocate, it is imperative to identify the ways in which institutional, structural, and interpersonal racism shows up so that we can work as we must to actively dismantle all forms.

Defining Activism

For the purpose of the handbook, activism is defined as efforts in which individuals or groups seek to make a change to the status quo for the benefit of oppressed groups and oppressive systemic structures.[14] Activists have strived to bring awareness to the social injustice that emphasizes direct, vigorous action, especially in support of, or opposition to, one side of a controversial issue.[15]

Activism as a tool for social change has historically been effective in raising awareness and facilitating change and has evolved into diverse engagement in activities striving to bring about political and social transformation. Activism has changed over time, and in the 21st century has taken on new forms, but the purpose and reason for activism have held steady and may be displayed in the form of marches, protests, forums, discussions, and education.[16]

Today, activism has expanded and also occurs through social media with the utilization of hashtags, Facebook posts, and 140-character tweets, birthing social movements by instantly reaching the masses. Activism continues to be a forum where people, in the face of disagreement, are utilizing their voices, speaking truth to power, and speaking truth to the public. This is why activism still matters today.

Activism on College Campuses

Sampson and Korn[17] described student activists as those who exist in a complex ecosystem, suspended in two worlds within themselves. By virtue of being students, student activists exist in a contemplative world of scholarly thought, rooted in tradition and academic order. And by embodying an activist identity, student activists also exist in a world of challenging policy and decision-making, where choices are made by altruism, centering values first. The uniqueness of their positionality can cause a great deal of cognitive dissonance and dissension within themselves as they navigate in two worlds. College campuses are microcosms of society, and due to the continuous injustices of Black, marginalized, and other communities of color, a rise in campus activism has occurred.

Campus activism in the 1960s, portraying the epic power of student coalition-building, made history that present-day campus activism has replicated as a means to advocate for social justice. Black students began to recognize a shift in rising Black consciousness of the Civil Rights Movement to Black Power.[18] Furthermore, when a collective mass of individuals' consciousness is raised to injustices that occur in their community, they are empowered to leave a legacy and uplift their community to demand equity and equality.

As an illustration of present-day activism, political strategist Rye[19] offered an operational definition of activism in which she coined the term *working woke*. Closely tied to activist Charles Hamilton's statement in a keynote address to Black Student Unions in 1968, "People don't talk revolution, they do revolution,"[20] Rye recognized the notion of being "woke" (i.e., conscious) of the injustices in society but postulated the crucial need to respond to and engage in activism—hence, "working woke." Each new generation of student activists creates new and divergent ways to change the landscape of higher education and how decision-makers must address student activism and advocacy. Without creativity, innovation, and against-the-norm approaches, campus activism efforts may be halted by administration, staff, and those opposed to such public tactics before the efforts can take hold and launch.[21] Nonetheless, they persist.

> *Everyone is needed. This is the fight for our lives.*

The 2016 Millennial Impact Report (MIR) revealed that 36% of students participated in at least one demonstration in the last month before the report. What was a factor that provoked many of these protests and demonstrations? The 2016 election result. Those students who did not initially support Trump were becoming vocal by using activism to respond to high-profile social issues. In the same manner, 86% of students expressed that they could make a difference, and 81% were confident that those actions would lead to improvements.[22]

The results of the 2015 Higher Education Research Institute's Cooperative Institutional Research Program (CIRP) Freshman Survey indicated a rise in student activism on campuses across the nation, the highest figure in the survey's 50-year existence. One in 10 incoming first-year students expected to participate in student protests while in college.[23] Black students (16%) were twice as likely to say that they would join campus protests as were white students (7.1%).[24] This trend continued as the climate of the nation became even more divided. The 2019 Freshman Survey found that 72.2% of students considered getting involved in causes of social justice as an essential part of their academic journey.[25] Academic institutions are a crucial component of activism, and students have an impact on the culture and climate of their college campuses.[26] The current generation of students leading the Black Lives Matter movement is reminiscent of students fiercely exercising their activism in the 1960s, answering the call to social justice.[27]

Integrating Campus Activism with the Community

Activism and social movements have been displayed on college campuses in partnership with the greater community throughout the decades.[28] Because of the reality of the oppressive structures in both higher education and society, students have diverged from the status quo to engage in a variety of forms of activism; they have organized lunch counter sit-ins, created conferences and coalitions, engaged in protests, occupied spaces, utilized media, and collaborated with community, civil rights activists, and college athletes to demand change.[29]

A very specific type of social movement called "new emotional movements" have come to the forefront of society. These movements come into existence after highly publicized events of random and senseless violence or are, more generally, directly reacting to a "suddenly imposed grievance."[30] For example, the societal triggers of the Black Campus Movement that occurred during the Civil Rights Movement in 1965 were two monumental events that shook society: (a) the assassination of Malcolm X on February 21, 1965, and (b) only two weeks later on March 7, 1965, the March on Selma for voting rights for African Americans, also known as Bloody Sunday because of the inhumane treatment and beating of Black bodies by law enforcement.[31]

These two moments galvanized the Black community to continue to organize and agitate against white supremacist structures on college campuses as well as in society. This in turn formed the Black Panther Party (originally titled the Black Panther Party for Self-Defense), which was born in 1966 in Oakland, CA. Huey P. Newton and Bobby Seale, both students at Merritt College, were dissatisfied with the progress of the Civil Rights Movement for the Black community. The students used their experiences working with a variety of Black power organizations and founded the Black Panther Party, the most influential Black movement in history.[32]

The Black Panther Party challenged police brutality; sought to protect the Black community by launching neighborhood patrols; provided educational, legal, and transportation assistance; and included the Free Breakfast for Children Program that spread to every major American city with a Black Panther Party chapter.[33] The Black Panther Party's ten-point program outlined the organizers' principal stance, with demands rooted in equality and justice.

Some of the most prominent activists worked alongside Newton and Seale in the Black Panther Party. These individuals included Fred Hampton, Eldridge and Kathleen Cleaver, Stokely Carmichael, and Angela Davis.[34] With chapters in several major American cities, the Black Panther Party laid the foundation for social movements like the Women's Movement, the Gay Rights Movement, the Environmental Movement, the Mills College strike, the Chicano Studies Movement, and many others.[35] Students on college campuses have been an integral part of each movement's support throughout the nation.[36] What happens within the walls of higher education is indeed a microcosm of society.

A modern example of this type of social movement is the Black Lives Matter (BLM) movement that was sparked as a result of the lynching of unarmed Black bodies at the hands of police and armed civilians.[37] The BLM movement originated as a Black-centered political will- and movement-building project but has flourished into a chapter-based, member-led organization whose mission is to build local power and intervene when violence is inflicted on Black communities by the state and vigilantes.[38]

In the BLM, like the Black Panther Party and the Civil Rights Movement, justice and equality for all is the foundation of the movement. This movement took a galvanizing turn in the summer of 2020 as diverse communities engaged in protests in every single state in America after the murders of George Floyd, Ahmaud Arbery, Breonna Taylor, and Elijah Jovan McClain, which was followed two months later by the shooting in the back of unarmed Jacob Blake by the police. All these protests proclaimed this simple civil right—that all Black lives matter, and this became a rallying cry for unifying a society broken by racism.

Activism and Social Justice

Lynn and Dixson[39] defined social justice as efforts aimed at providing equal distribution of rights, privileges, opportunities, and resources within a society. Feagin[40] defined social justice as a redistribution of resources from those who have unjustly gained them to those who justly deserve them; it also means creating and ensuring the processes of truly democratic participation in decision-making. Feagin also stated that social justice requires resource equity, fairness, and respect for diversity, as well as the eradication of existing forms of social oppression.

The Center for Economic and Social Justice asserted in 2018 that social justice imposes on each of us a personal responsibility to work with others to design and continually perfect our institutions as tools for personal and social development. Individuals committed to social justice are those who actively work toward institutional and social change and are knowledgeable about and aware of how their own racial identities influence their interactions with others. They also have a greater understanding of individual and institutional racism and how their racial identities may impact institutional decisions, policies, and interactions with people from diverse backgrounds.[41]

The commitment for social change has largely been viewed as the responsibility of oppressed people and disenfranchised groups.[42] However, in order for the needle to truly move, equality and equity for all must be a collective effort and force to dismantle hatred, racism, and all forms of oppression.

Where is your calling in the fight for social justice?

_____

_____

_____

_____

So, you've had a quick history lesson—now what?

CHAPTER TWO

Introducing the Activism Growth Model™ (AGM)

"Write what you want to read."
—*Toni Morrison*

The increased activism and advocacy on college campuses and in communities has led to a surge of individuals desiring to step boldly into their activist and advocate identities. As exciting as this epiphany can be, it can also lead to a feeling of fear, trepidation, and the "imposter syndrome," which is defined as the feeling that you aren't worthy of contributing, that your voice and experiences are fraudulent. With this epiphany, some have also experienced feelings of not knowing exactly how, when, where, or with whom to engage and develop their advocate or activist identity. This can lead to a feeling of despair or a lack of direction, with so much passion and uncertainty about which path to take to fuel your fire. I can relate. I've been there.

I write this pregnant with my first child, a beautiful and free Black baby boy, at home in the middle of a global pandemic. And as I feel every kick, twitch, and roll he makes in my body, I feel empowered because during the summer of 2020, my activism was birthing Black life, a revolutionary action. Watching the world being set on fire by tired, angry, and exhausted Black and African American people with their non-Black allies, and accomplices, I felt joy, sadness, empowerment, and despair. I wanted deeply to be in the streets with my people because marching and protesting is one of my vehicles of choice when I have engaged in activism over the years.

I felt their pain. I was tired of seeing another Black brother or sister being lynched by law enforcement, and seemingly nothing was taking place systemically. I was taken right back many years ago to the feeling of wondering, What can I do during this time? How else can I stand in solidarity with my community of activists to speak truth to power? My call to share this labor of love right at this moment became so blatantly clear; it was time to introduce the Activism Growth Model™ (AGM).

I created the AGM to be a guide as you embark on your journey to engage in activism and advocacy. The goals of this model are to continuously center the experiences and narratives of individuals of color in times of racial and social injustice. Equally as important, the model provides strategies used through my journey and those I have worked with over the years to help empower you. As this model has continued to flourish, not only does it continue to serve Black, Indigenous, and People of Color (BIPOC) and communities, it has also expanded to individuals of privilege and diverse communities who have experienced a heightened sense of calling to engage in activism and advocacy as well. My hope is that this framework can be useful as you navigate your campus and your community and build upon your advocacy and activism to overcome barriers you may face as you speak truth to power and develop your calling and voice.

Research that Informed the Activism Growth Model™

There were multiple studies that I conducted over the years, and from those findings, I built the pillars and cornerstones of the AGM. The first study was my dissertation titled "Love Is at the Root of the Resistance: A Hermeneutic Phenomenological Inquiry into the Lived Experiences of Black College Athlete Activists," where I captured the lived experiences of Black College Athlete Activists (BCAAs) in times of racial and social injustice. I spent a year with nine dynamic Black and African American young men, women, and individuals from Division 1 schools from across the United States who shared their experiences in the intersections of their identities as they grew, developed, and leaned into their activist identities. I will go into more detail on this study later in the book as I share the model designed specifically for stakeholders to engage and empower BCAAs and Activists of Color.

Next, I had the pleasure of working with 27 Black and African American young men, women, and individuals who identified as athletes, student leaders, or both at a small liberal arts, faith-based institution on the West Coast. As I spent time with these intriguing students, they were passionate about leading not just on their teams, but in the community and in different realms on campus. I conducted surveys and focus groups to hear about whether the experiences of individuals were authentically aligning with the mission and vision of the constitution, especially because the Black student population was less than 3%.

The third study that informed my findings involved six female doctoral students of color navigating their Ph.D.s in a higher education program at a large West Coast, faith-based institution. These women were incredibly multifunctional in their identities as students, mothers, partners, caregivers, and helping professionals at institutions in higher education across the United States. Witnessing and hearing their narratives and stories about how they were growing and utilizing their voices in a multitude of ways was so inspirational. I have learned and continue to learn from these tenacious women.

For my fourth study, I was invited to a student leader retreat known as The Movement at a large, public, California State University. A long-standing and thriving force on campus, The Movement was composed of leaders of all Black and African American clubs, organizations, and groups on their campus as well as active mentorship from the Black faculty and staff association. Focus groups were conducted with 30 student leaders, both undergraduate and graduate, who identified as activists or advocates, illustrating a consciousness of issues that affect the Black/African American community and a desire to be part of a community of empowerment and change. On- and off-campus student leadership and participation varied from identity-based clubs and organizations to religious or spiritual leadership or mentorship. In addition to centering their narratives as activists and advocates on campus and in their communities, this student population identified and called for accountability in the support and resources they desired from higher education practitioners and stakeholders.

The last study was the study of myself, known as an autoethnography. In research, an autoethnography is a form of qualitative research in which an author uses self-reflection and writing to explore anecdotal and personal experience to connect this autobiographical story to wider cultural, political, and social meanings and understandings.[43] Through my path, I've collected voice notes, journal entries, videos, social media posts, papers, assignments, and reflections; watched videos of my parents and their journey; as well as met with people in my village as they have received my journey and growth in activism. In other words, I researched the entire internal and external ecosystem I've navigated over the years.

Honoring My Scholar Activist Ancestors: Theories that Ground the Activist Growth Model™

As a researcher and scholar activist, I pay homage to those scholar activists before me who have created powerful and captivating models and theories that inspired the foundation of the Activist Growth Model™. The first guiding theory that informed the foundation of the AGM is critical race theory (CRT).[44] Critical race theory is used to study and theorize about the intersection of race, racism, and power that strives to uncover how white supremacy and its oppression of people of color has been established and perpetuated.

Critical race theory has seven tenets that shape the framework, which are: (a) commitment to social justice, (b) permanence of racism, (c) experiential knowledge (counternarratives), (d) intersectionality, (e) interest convergence, (f) whiteness as a property, and (g) critique of liberalism.[45] Although the theory has seven tenets, the AGM was guided by the four tenets of counternarratives, intersectionality, commitment to social justice, and the permanence of racism.

As aforementioned, centering the narratives of the activists and advocates who I've worked with over the years is the cornerstone for all of the work I have done and will ever do, and this book is no exception. This is particularly important because, depending on the spaces that individuals resided in and navigated through, their voices weren't seen as valid or accepted as aligning with the white or Eurocentric normative voice or experience. Therefore, my goal in the creation of the AGM is to not only honor and center their narratives, but to be intentional in the recognition of all of their identities and those narratives.

> *It was incredible and beautiful to witness and hear of these stories of resistance and the dismantling of such systems.*

Not only were these individuals I learned from in my research Black, they also identified as being a part of the LGBTQIA community, male, female, gender nonconforming, representing a multitude of religious or spiritual dispositions, immigrants, those with salient or invisible disabilities or exceptionalities and so many more backgrounds, embodying intersectionality.

As their identities coexisted to make up the fabric of who they are, their commitment to social justice was clear and apparent. The permanence of racism is the last tenet in critical race theory that served as the foundation of the AGM when working with activists and advocates. We wholeheartedly know that we do not live in a post-racist society—it was blatant and clear as experiences of racism dripped through their narratives.

The second theory and model that provided foundation to the AGM is Yosso's[46] Community Cultural Wealth. According to this model, there are six types of capital that are nurtured by BIPOC and communities that collectively form cultural wealth. This model is profound as it aligns with the AGM because the types of capital are considered gems for BIPOC students and individuals.

They bring these gems to the table as they grow and develop into their advocate and activist identities on their campuses and in their communities. These gems were so perfectly articulated in the experiences of the individual paths that led to their activist identities. Yosso posits that these capitals are gems of strength, especially when certain spaces they navigate in aren't seen as welcoming to their identities and their voices and their experiences aren't seen as valid or recognized, causing oppression.

There are six types of capital represented in the theory of community cultural wealth; however, the AGM is guided by these four in particular: aspirational capital, familial capital, social capital, and resistant capital.

- The aspirational capital posits that individuals continue to strive to honor their ancestors in thought, word, and deed as activists and advocates, aspiring to be the best versions of themselves. They aim high in their goals, dreams, and desires as BIPOC.

- The familial capital is symbolized by recognizing and bringing the traditions their family and culture has taught them into their activism at all levels on campus and in the community. This was illustrated in many ways. As for me, I found myself reading the books and listening to the records and songs my parents left for me that spoke so deeply to the importance of Black resistance, education, and empowerment.

> *As I earned my Ph.D., I aspired to make my parents proud and now to make my son proud as Doctor Mama, by speaking up and using my voice for the voiceless to create a more just and humane world for him to grow up in.*

- The social capital emphasizes the awareness of the importance of being a part of social communities that strengthen causes, especially as they navigate dominantly white institutions and dominantly white spaces. These social communities can be big or small, on a worldwide scale or as a part of local support groups. They bring rejuvenation and respite, providing spaces for solidarity in one's journey.

- The resistant capital is the embodiment of what the Activist Growth Model™ exemplifies. Boldly resisting and infiltrating spaces that were never created with BIPOC in mind, nonetheless, we resist, we organize, and continue to dismantle white supremacy. Although a great many of the individuals I worked with in my research were connected to education in one way, shape, or form, almost every institution can be shown to have been created to cater to the white, male, Christian, able-bodied, middle- and upper-class entities. I felt empowered to reflect on my journey of resistance, and it was incredible and beautiful to witness and hear of these stories of resistance and the dismantling of such systems that built the foundation of this book.

The second-to-last theory guiding the foundation of the AGM is Black Feminist Thought (BFT).[47] Collins emphasizes the perspectives of African American women and by utilizing BFT as a conceptual research framework, Black and African American women activists and scholars can rearticulate a Black women's standpoint by being rooted in the everyday experiences of African American women.[48]

Black Feminist Thought empowers them with the right to interpret their reality and define their experiences.[49] This framework is so poignant when examining interlocking systems of oppression that take place every single day, systems that permeate through the narratives of the Black and African American women I studied.

The major characteristics of BFT are (a) the lived experience as a criterion of meaning, and (b) using dialogue in assessing knowledge claims.[50] These two characteristics align with the goals of my research, the AGM, and provided a powerful framework in articulating my position as a Black woman, scholar, and activist cultivating this work.

The last theory and model that guided the AGM is Maslow's Hierarchy of Needs.[51] As a psychology and counseling major, Maslow's Hierarchy of Needs was one of the first theories that I learned in my educational journey, and I continue to utilize this theory in my research and teaching, as well as when I counsel individuals and groups. Maslow's Hierarchy of Needs is a motivational theory in psychology that demonstrates the building of one's foundation before moving to the next stage to develop toward what Maslow refers to as self-actualization.

The AGM labels that as being a holistic activist or advocate. The AGM is inspired by the visual conceptualization of the hierarchy of needs—each step or phase in building one's activist identity will give you the foundation, resources, and tools toward becoming a holistic activist or advocate.

Grounding the Activist Growth Model™ in theory as well as practice not only incorporates my background as a researcher, but illustrates the importance of the practicality of this model, demonstrating that this model can be utilized in educational spheres as well as in the social justice community. Therefore, wherever you are on the spectrum to activate change in your calling and duty to engage in activism:

> *"Do it! What are you waiting on? Do it!*
> *Stand up for what you believe in.*
> *The world needs your voice.*
> *Whoever you are, you have something to say.*
> *Say it."*
> *—Kerry Washington*

CHAPTER THREE

Tenets of the Activism Growth Model™

In my years of counseling and teaching individuals, groups, and communities, I've taken a strengths-based cognitive behavioral approach. In counseling and psychology, this is where helping professionals assist individuals with discovering positive aspects about themselves and their internal strengths, thus increasing their motivation to want to make changes in their lives. Padesky[52] includes four steps in the strengths-based cognitive behavioral approach, which is (a) search, (b) construct, (c) apply, and (d) practice.

In the tenets of the AGM, these steps are incorporated as I assist you while you dig deeply into your:

(a) Soul work

(b) Discovery of your role or roles

(c) Activism vehicles for your role to operate in

(d) Search for your community

(e) Understanding of the barriers and obstacles to your activism

(f) Prioritizing of practicing radical self-care

We will unpack each tenet through defining it, providing examples of the tenet through the experiences of the dynamic activists I have worked with through the years, and giving examples of poignant figures throughout history. I will also share my personal stories as they align with each tenet.

Activism Growth Model™

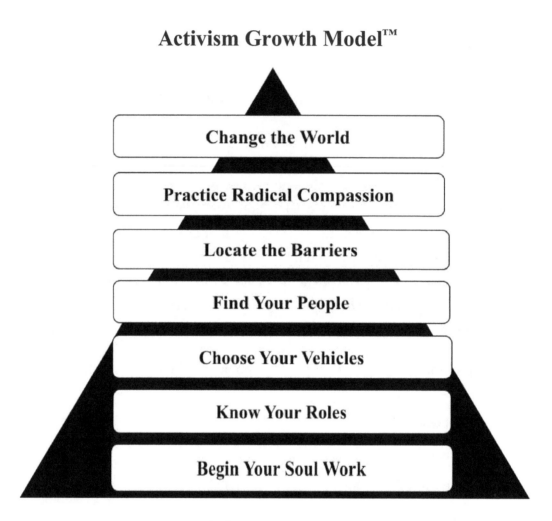

Change the World

Practice Radical Compassion

Locate the Barriers

Find Your People

Choose Your Vehicles

Know Your Roles

Begin Your Soul Work

© George-Williams, 2020

CHAPTER FOUR

Begin Your Soul Work

This is the foundation of the model and where the inner work begins. As you continue to find your calling to advocacy and activism, this is the place where you identify personal and social triggers, or antecedents, that may reside within you. As you connect with your soul and calling, investigate your motivation for this work and take bold steps toward identifying where and if healing must take place to overcome internal fears and barriers. Writing this book, I recognize that we reside in such a heartbreakingly unique space. The year 2020 had the world suspended in the midst of two pandemics, COVID-19 and racism.

The global pandemic known as COVID-19, a viral disease that has affected people of all ages and ethnicities, has disproportionately plagued the Black and brown communities at much higher rates than white communities. Many argue that this is due to the inequities in the social determinants of health, such as poverty and healthcare access, which influence a wide range of health and quality-of-life outcomes and risks.[53] This virus has caused the world to pause and shelter in place while causing minoritized populations even more angst as the target is on their health and mortality. Consequently, as the world pauses, society has a front row to witnessing another pandemic that has been spreading for centuries—racism.

As both of these pandemics run rampant right before our eyes, it has a different effect on Black, Indigenous, and People of Color (BIPOC). COVID-19 commands us to stay put, while racism calls us to move, speak up, and not sit idly by as another Black body succumbs to death by racism. These two dynamics most certainly cause major internal conflict. If there is conflict happening within you, take a moment to do a self-inventory.

Ask yourself: Where is that conflict resonating within you? Take a moment to recognize this and investigate where it is residing in your mind, body, and soul.

_____

_____

_____

_____

Those who are reading this book feel compelled to move and identify strategies, tools, and resources to engage in activism, but first we must identify the pain of these pandemics and the pain of personal or societal triggers, then locate where the healing must take place. That is soul work.

> *Discovering who you are in the fight for social justice is deepening, enlivening, and invigorating.*

This generation of students and members of the community employ not only the passion the activist ancestors of the 1960s embodied, but also the keen awareness of the platforms they have to speak out from for those in disenfranchised identities and groups, many which they personally embody. Eager to engage and empower others, the activists I worked with shared how personal intersecting identities serve as individual antecedents to activism and how those intersections shape their experiences. Some shared that their motivation, triggers, or antecedents to engage in activism and use their voice did not always emerge quickly, but rather over an extended period of time through a variety of avenues. While some experienced an overwhelming sense of urgency to act, these antecedents or triggers, both individual and external societal critical moments, ultimately led participants to actualize their activism.

For instance, after seeing the tragedy unfold in Ferguson, MO, and the aftermath of the murdering of Mike Brown by law enforcement, and other personal experiences of racism on her campus, Ariyana Smith, a player on the Knox College women's basketball team and arguably the first college athlete activist of the Black Lives Matter movement, took a stand against injustice.[54] On November 29, 2014, during the national anthem, Smith walked over to the flag in the gymnasium with her hands up in the "don't shoot" gesture and dropped to the floor before the flag. She laid there for 4 minutes and 30 seconds in protest of the police killing of teenager Mike Brown and leaving his body lying in the street in Ferguson, MO, for 4½ hours.

In any fight for justice, one's consciousness is raised to the perils of society especially as it pertains to one's identity. Blair, a young Black woman, political science major, athlete, leader in her community, and self-identified activist, was not shy of critical incidents and moments that were not only painful, but also transformative, centering around her race. Her upbringing consisted of many moments of being the only Black girl in white spaces, resulting in feeling isolation. Her upbringing was in a predominantly white environment where she frequently faced racism:

> *"When I was young, I was the only Black girl in class and kids would say, 'You can't play with us because you're Black'.... In high school, I remember I went to one party with my friend one time and then the guy of the house was like 'don't bring anyone if they're Black. This party is for white people only.' It was that awareness of, if you cannot accept my people and where I came from, but you are going to accept me because I am different or whatever, that is not okay with me. Because of incidents like those, I separated myself from being with only my white friends and started branching out and meeting other people of color."*

Because Blair experienced onlyness and racism in her upbringing, her call to activism only expanded once she got to college and leaned into her activist identity.

Austin, a young man earning his degree in a large state institution in Southern California was from the city in Florida where Trayvon Martin resided and was murdered. Trayvon's death struck a chord and galvanized the country, overflowing into the consciousness of generations of BIPOC and activists who became deeply compelled to mobilize and ignite a nation. Experiencing the beginning of such a movement and living in close proximity to the injustice of Trayvon Martin's murder, Austin reflected on how Trayvon's death affected his activism:

> "I attended the same school as Trayvon Martin, and I witnessed how everything exploded from there. I had a perspective that was fairly different, as I actually knew of Trayvon. And then I go back to school and we see all of these news cameras, and we find out a student from the school was killed. Then I hear it's Trayvon Martin. And I'm like, I've seen his face before. I remember hearing the police call, and you hear all the screams in the background, and the gunfire. And all I could do is just cry…. As a Black male, just seeing how this stuff occurred and he's from the same area, being born and raised in Miami Gardens. I knew right then, I've got to do something. I don't like to be the one who constantly talks about problems and then just goes away. I've got to be about action."

Many of the activists I worked with also reflected on their family's foundation of deep roots in activism, allowing them to be confident in their activism. Logan, a senior student leader, volleyball player, history major, and community activist has deep roots in activism for generations before her:

> "My mom is very into politics, and she is one of those super outspoken types of people. My uncle has a political and law background, which I identify with, especially about the state statutes, the law, and the constitutions. My grandma would always talk about her marching with Dr. King and had pictures of it, so I feel like that was pretty cool to see and hear about her stories. Also, my aunt has always been active as well. She went to protests and marches with my grandma and still goes to every march and does everything."

As I was earning my master's degree and then my Ph.D., I actively engaged in discovering and rediscovering my "why" to continue to stay connected to my core and investigate my soul work and purpose. After my mother passed away in 2018, to celebrate her first heavenly birthday, I honored her by inviting my family and loved ones to share stories of my mother, many of which I had never heard and some oldies but goodies of how her life impacted not just my family, but her students and seemingly anyone she met. She embodied beauty in her Blackness and was a leader in so many realms in her career and personal life. I heard more stories of how she advocated for disadvantaged students and families, as well as many instances of how she jeopardized her status as a tenured teacher to serve as a strike leader in the 1989 Los Angeles Unified School District (LAUSD) strike.

Those memories intertwined with stories of my father's radicalism and how they both engaged in activism in different ways throughout their lives. A loved one would say to me, "You are your daddy's daughter with your activism, unapologetic in all your ways, but the love and tenderness you have for your students and all who you mentor, that's all your mama." I recorded those sessions and took quotes from that day that now serve as screensavers and notes in my office to always remind me that I am honoring my family by continuing their legacy and creating a space for my own path toward social justice.

I encourage you to engage in exercises like writing in a journal or jotting down your motivations somewhere to make them visible, to keep your calling accountable, and to keep your energy in times of peril. As you continue to do your soul work, and as your motivation and calling emerges, rejuvenates or is revitalized, I invite you to reflect on these questions.

Questions to Ask Yourself: Soul Work

What is your definition of activism and advocacy?

_____

_____

_____

_____

Why are you called to serve as an activist and advocate?

_____

_____

_____

_____

Why now?

_____

_____

_____

_____

How has your mindset changed, grown, developed, or expanded?

_____

_____

_____

_____

What community or communities are you called to serve and to be an activist and advocate for?

_____

_____

_____

_____

What topics or issues compel you to lean into your advocacy and activism? Why?

_____

_____

_____

_____

What (if any) personal injustices that have taken place in your life show up in your calling toward social justice and advocacy?

_____

_____

_____

_____

What injustices endure in the communities you identify with, and how do those injustices affect your calling toward social justice and advocacy?

_____

_____

_____

_____

What are the active ways you have begun, or will begin, the healing from those personal or communal injustices? (A few examples of this can look like therapy, counseling, journaling, support groups, or any safe space where healing can be released to do the authentic work you are called to do.)

_____

_____

_____

_____

Soul work is not only emotional weightlifting, but the body also experiences growing pains, and you owe it to yourself to care for your mind, body, and soul. Discovering who you are in the fight for social justice is deepening, enlightening, and invigorating. Therefore, taking the time to investigate your calling and healing through soul work is the first and foundational tenet of the Activism Growth Model™.

CHAPTER FIVE

Know Your Roles

"The most common way people give up their power is
by thinking they don't have any."
—Alice Walker

You are the architect of your destiny. As you navigate this space of discovery, rediscovery, and a deepened sense of calling toward activism, what are you wired to do? Just as activism is defined a multitude of ways, the roles of activism also have many identities. For the sake of the Activism Growth Model™, the roles of activism are defined as: (a) agitator, (b) reformer, (c) change agent, and (d) versatile activist.

Agitators

Throughout the years as I discovered, grew, and developed my activist identity and calling, I have engaged in diverse roles in activism. However, the times when I have engaged in the agitator role are where the core of my calling is. To be honest, it's the role where I've had the most fun! I have always operated with a sense of urgency in all I am passionate about, and those who are called toward the agitator role put issues on society's agenda through dramatic, nonviolent actions. Agitators are urgent about making a difference while exhibiting an unapologetic energy toward that approach.

Author, activist, and scholar bell hooks, in *Writing Beyond Race: Living Theory and Practice*, gives a poignant definition of agitation as a "meaningful resistance to dominator culture, which demands of all of us a willingness to accurately identify the various systems that work together to promote injustice, exploitation, and oppression."[55] As the most misunderstood role of activists, agitators are important to the family of activism because they prevent society from ignoring or denying a violation of widely held values. Because of this, a widespread misconception that is

29

associated with the agitator role is that when people think of an activist, they only envision the agitator because this role is typically the role media and anti-activists love to vilify. They see the agitator as someone who is "disrupting" the status quo. But I ask, whose status is it disrupting and making uncomfortable? Essentially, the agitation role of activism is for the purpose of disrupting the system or systems by acting individually or as a group to bring the grievances of specific individuals or groups to the forefront of public awareness.

The vehicles through which agitators and all those carrying activist roles commonly utilize are multifaceted and will be unpacked in more detail in Chapter Six. Nonetheless, I have had the pleasure of seeing the diversity in approaches that agitators operate in from those throughout history, individuals I have worked with in my research, and from my personal experience in the agitator role.

I had the pleasure of mentoring some student leaders and members of a group of Black, Indigenous, and People of Color (BIPOC) and LGBTQIA undergraduate and graduate agitators. They were at their wits' end with the administration after multiple attempts to meet with them to share their grievances and concerns about being microaggressed or experiencing blatant incidents of racism on campus. They formed a group called Decolonize the University, demanding that diversity and inclusivity must extend beyond the Center for Multicultural Services and the Office of Diversity and Inclusivity, and that all students deserve a quality education free of discrimination from educators and administration alike.

> *They were tired of sitting idly by and waiting for the administration to take notice as they followed "protocol" by submitting social justice incident reports online to no avail.*

It was time for them to ignite the agitator in themselves. The students occupied the building where the offices of the president, provost, some deans, and higher-level administrators were on the same floor. They all covered their mouths with tape as a symbol that their voices, experiences, and identities were silenced on campus and held signs demanding a more inclusive campus. The activism vehicle they used as agitators was known as a public display or symbolic form of activism, which will be detailed later in Chapter Six.

After no responses from administrators, the group occupied the faculty senate meeting while live-streaming the event on social media. Were the members of the faculty senate welcoming, attentive, and empathetic to students interrupting their meeting by sharing their experiences of being microaggressed by some of their faculty colleagues? Of course not. The exchanges between the faculty senate and students went viral, and the students in the Decolonize the University group's agitator tactics put the university on notice.

From there they created a www.change.org petition articulating their demands. The petition called for mandatory faculty and staff training on diversity and inclusion, revamping of the Eurocentric curriculum, cultural competency as a part of the tenure evaluation process, and the creation of a Minority Postdoctoral Fellowship Program to recruit and retain more faculty of color, among other demands. Shortly after the demonstrations went viral, an incident of racial and sexual harassment on social media targeting the Black and Latinx women in the group took place, further galvanizing the students to intensify actions to publicly call out the president and administrators, who had remained silent.

The last act of agitation the group engaged in was the most public act—airing grievances of what was taking place on campus. They reached out to news outlets, the NAACP, and other social justice groups, asking them to attend their public demonstration. They invited current students and alums to share personal stories of microaggressions, incidents of tokenism, and acts of racism by the president, administration, faculty, other students, and staff dating back years. They even had emails and letters from those who were unable to attend and they read each one aloud at the demonstration. It was truly powerful. These young men and women exhibited the agitator role with intention, urgency, and excellence. The Decolonize the University group left an impact on how the university navigates issues of racism and microaggressions, and how it formally embraces equity for all students.

The Legacy of Malcolm X and Others

An example of an agitator ancestor is Malcolm X. He was born Malcolm Little and was better known as Malcolm X after converting to the Nation of Islam, adopting the last name "X" to represent his rejection of his "slave" name and to represent his lost tribe name. He was a prolific minister, orator, and human rights activist who occupied a unique and necessary space during the Civil Rights Movement as the more radical entity on the spectrum of social justice for the Black and African American community. He embodied the agitator role because his stance often put him at odds with the nonviolent teachings of Martin Luther King, Jr.

Malcolm X urged his fellow Black Americans to protect themselves against white aggression and white supremacy "by any means necessary," and wholeheartedly believed in Black self-defense. In fact, activist ancestor Ida B. Wells, who died in 1931, paved the way for such a stance as she proclaimed, "A Winchester rifle should have a place of honor in every black home, and it should be used for that protection which the law refuses to give."

Malcolm X certainly had no qualms with unapologetically indicting white America for its crimes against Black Americans, calling out systemic injustices on public platforms whenever and wherever he saw fit. He spoke to a growing part of the Black and African American community that Fannie Lou Hamer in 1964 referred to as "*sick and tired of being sick and tired*" of the disenfranchisement, criminalization, lynching, and oppression of their fellow Black brothers and sisters.

Malcolm X occupied the stance of preventing society from ignoring or denying a violation of widely held values that all men and women are created equal. At the height of the Civil Rights Movement, there was no wavering in his agitator role and approach and no ends to which he and his constituents felt must take place to dismantle white supremacy. I highly recommend the book *The Autobiography of Malcolm X*, which chronicles his life and views on race, religion, and Black nationalism. It has been a bestseller for decades and continues to shape the minds and hearts of activists everywhere.

Amanda Seales, a multi-hyphenated public figure and juggernaut, especially to the Black community, embodies an agitator role in all the spaces she inhabits. A comedian, actress, podcaster, author, artist, songwriter, DJ, poet, entrepreneur, and media personality holding a master's degree in African American Studies with a concentration in Hip-Hop from Columbia University, Amanda has unapologetically carved out spaces to not only celebrate Blackness, but to continuously call out inequitable spaces in Hollywood and in the larger community. She recently disclosed that she left a co-host role on the daytime TV talk show *The Real* because of the lack of Black producers and the attempt of executive producers to silence her voice in discussing issues that directly affect the Black community on the show, calling for accountability in diversity in leadership of programming.

Hosting the first-ever virtual Black Entertainment Television (BET) Awards show the summer of 2020, Seales spoke about the killings of all the Black individuals at the hands of police and particularly about the lack of sanctions for the officers who murdered Breonna Taylor, who was shot multiple times while sleeping in her own bed after an unauthorized raid on her house. In every platform Seales occupies and through multiple avenues, either through her social media outlets, her podcast, interviews, or her own book, she carries an agitator energy coupled with an educational background to bring grievances afflicting the Black community to light and demand urgency toward social justice.

> *Activism operates on many roads and in many realms.*

As an agitator, it is important to know that you may reach your destination of putting a grievance in a public sphere and raising awareness of the injustice or injustices, but ultimately the major goal may not be attainable solely in the agitator role. Here's an example of reaching the destination but not yet obtaining the goal: The protests that stirred the world during the COVID-19 quarantine of 2020 caused a heightened awareness of the racism, inequalities, and police brutality that still plague minoritized groups. The protests were necessary to bring about the awareness of such injustices; however, racism, inequalities, and police brutality have not been abolished yet. The agitators at the forefront of these protests were crucial to begin the process for the family of activists to lean into their calling to take the baton to continue the work to dismantle these systems in the reformer and change agent roles. That is why as an agitator, it is imperative to celebrate all the victories in raising awareness of injustices and operating with the unapologetic energy to do so.

In some instances, agitation can be just the fire to reach the destination and accomplish the goals. For example, consider the case of Cyntoia Brown, the young woman who was sentenced to life in prison at age 16 for murdering a man and claiming self-defense because she believed he was going to kill her. Despite being only 16 at the time of the killing, she was tried as an adult and ended up serving 15 years in prison. The agitator role was in full effect in 2017 when Brown's case went viral following the intervention of several high-profile celebrities and activists who used their social media to express outrage over her sentence and to bring about awareness of the heinous inequities and cracks in the criminal justice system.

Celebrities like Rihanna, Kim Kardashian, T.I., Snoop Dogg, Angela Rye, and LeBron James posted about this case. After the details of Brown's conviction became viral, her case was reopened and she was ultimately granted clemency in 2019. This is a perfect example of a time when agitation to heighten awareness of her case as well as of inequities in the criminal justice system not only was the goal but reached the destination of getting Cyntoia Brown released from prison for time served.

Activism operates on many roads and in many realms. As I share examples of activists on campuses and involved in the community, I also want to affirm that you can be an agitator in your own ecosystem. As you do your soul work, it can be apparent that some systems within your individual universe may need to be examined, disrupted, or eliminated. Remember, you have a sphere of influence no matter how big or small. I have experienced this, as well as witnessing loved ones whose decisions to seek therapy, speak up against archaic dynamics in their family, go away to college, or marry whoever the hell they wanted to marry or be with (just to name a few actions) have shaken and disrupted generational strongholds that have set them free in so many ways.

Bringing grievances up to the forefront of public awareness does not have to mean creating a petition or organizing a protest; it can also mean verbalizing and creating boundaries to your loved ones and promising to yourself that you will keep them. It can also mean standing up and advocating for yourself when experiencing personal injustices or inequities in your workplace or other spaces you inhabit. This is where the healing and examination of personal injustices can surface within yourself as you continue to do your soul work and discover who you are and your role in activism. A misconception of "successfully" engaging in activism is that one needs to have a large following on social media or hold multiple degrees, but I am here to tell you, good people, an agitator examines a system and decides as an individual that enough is enough.

What systems in your ecosystem do you feel the urgency to disrupt and change for the better or to make them more equitable?

_____

_____

_____

_____

A few weeks after I defended my dissertation, my classmates, alums, and I received word that one of our beloved faculty members was being let go from the university. The dean of the college claimed budget cuts while hiring a full-time professor months prior. This professor who was being let go was an integral part of a higher education program; she chaired and sat on ongoing dissertation committees, and was a beacon of love to many of the students. The chair of our program wasn't even on board with the firing of this professor because she too recognized how unfair the decision was, especially because the dean's reasoning wasn't truthful and transparent. I was furious.

I had personal qualms with this dean because he referred to me and another Black student as "causing trouble" when our cohort studied in South Africa the summer of

2017 because I used my voice to speak up against something I was not comfortable about during the trip. Therefore, when I heard that he made a knee-jerk decision to fire a pillar of our program, the agitator in me decided to come forth full throttle. As described, an agitator brings the grievances of specific individuals or groups to the forefront of public awareness, and that is exactly what I did.

I spoke with our program chair to gain more information on the decision and got her support to contact other alums or classmates to inform them of the professor's firing since many had not heard. I also informed her that I created a www.change.org petition demanding that the dean meet with us to articulate why he was releasing this professor and not the other professor who had only been a part of the university for a few months. I created social media posts and flyers, then called as well as emailed more than 100 alums, asking if they would share their experiences with this professor to illustrate the profound impact her departure would have on the program.

Worried about his reputation as an ineffective leader, the dean responded to me. His first tactic was to try to meet with me and other students individually, which I encouraged students to turn down, and I vehemently rejected this offer.

> *Activism 101: A critical mass is the more effective tactic when organizing and demanding change. One person could possibly be swayed, but a mass of righteous and like-minded individuals is a force to be reckoned with.*

As the agitator and organizer to demand the dean's accountability, I knew my role as an agitator, and I walked boldly in it. I was a self-identified activist throughout my journey as a doctoral student, so I knew I must utilize my leadership and activist skills to respond to an unjust situation involving someone I and many students cared about. If I didn't, I would be a hypocrite. That was one of those moments where I needed to be about that activist life.

As the mass of current students, alums, and other faculty members shared their support of our effort, we scheduled two virtual meeting sessions with the dean and the faculty chair so that students and alums could ask any questions regarding his decision and leadership. During these meetings, he squirmed and barely made eye contact with us, stuttered, and seemed defensive when we asked clarifying questions or caught him in a contradictory statement. We were all adults on the calls, working in the realms of higher education; therefore, we understood that decisions have to be made by the administration, but we most certainly did not trust his judgment.

The meetings did not produce more trust for his decision-making as a dean and a leader. As students and alums, we used our voices to share the disconnect we had with him. For example, the only time we would see this dean would be when he made some opening remarks at our graduation and perhaps one time walking to his office during the weeks we would be on campus. He apologized and vowed to be a more visible leader to our program. It wasn't the victory we desired because one of our favorite professors did not return, but he now knows that the Ph.D. students in the program demand higher accountability and transparency from their administrators. As the months followed, he did not forget about me—he made a comment at graduation about my activism when he announced my name. Yes indeed, I am about that agitator life, and he experienced it firsthand.

Lastly, if you feel compelled to walk in the calling of an agitator, I invite you to reflect on how you used your voice in the past during times when issues have grieved or upset you personally or have adversely affected groups or communities you feel passionate about supporting.

How comfortable did you feel in those moments?

_____

_____

_____

_____

Even if you experienced deep discomfort during those times, but still felt called and compelled to bring issues to the forefront, you were moving in your natural strength as an agitator, and now it's time to fully walk in your purpose.

Reformers

As you reflect on your intuitive solutions to problem-solving or when you see a problem or conflict arise, what is your immediate reaction to the solution? Do you seek out people in authority to attempt to correct the problem or conflict? Can you see yourself as someone who can be a part of the change or dismantling of a system by working within that system? If so, you are called to be a reformer. The reformer role is someone who works within structures to incorporate solutions into new laws and policies that will be accepted as the new conventional wisdom of society. In many instances, people in this role already have a position of leadership at their job or in their community, organization, or system, and work within that system or organization where they already have a voice. A reformer can also be someone who strives to step up to a leadership role to engage through activism to challenge those structures to become more equitable entities.

The climate of the nation and the world met a gruesome collision as we witnessed a Black man being murdered by white supremacists while taking a jog, another Black man murdered by strangulation from a cop kneeling on his neck, followed by the gut-wrenching news of a Black woman being shot multiple times while sleeping in her own bed by a wrong police raid. These events launched a swelling of protests that took place in every single state in America and in many countries. The protests produced a wave of companies, organizations, districts, and colleges posting "Black Lives Matter" on their homepages, sending mass emails with four- and five-paragraph statements proclaiming their stand with their Black patrons, employees, faculty, staff, students, and so forth.

This was a great start. However, reformers who are part of one of these entities publicly announcing their supposed support of Black lives may challenge these entities to release the numbers and percentages of BIPOC and LGBTQIA individuals they employ, as well as to reveal how many Black or African Americans are in leadership roles and how their salaries compare to their white counterparts. Disclosing this information would serve as a better indicator of whether BIPOC and LGBTQIA lives really matter to them.

As a scholar and activist on his campus and in his community, Austin utilized his voice and position to raise awareness and create sustained change. He not only utilized his platform in his community, but also engaged in leadership on campus, demonstrating activism at the individual level, influencing a system and policies, and infiltrating a space no Black student leader had occupied before him in student government in the dominantly white institution he attended in the Midwest. He reflected on his experience:

> *"I was the first Black college student to serve in student government*
> *at this level at this school. I wanted to be a voice for the Black student*
> *population here. I was on the leadership team, where we had a*
> *$42 million budget to control the finances for student organizations,*
> *and change the narrative and be influential in changing policies in*
> *our system."*

Austin engaged in the reformer role by utilizing his voice in student government as his presence created a space and lane for other Black students and community activists to assume more leadership roles. He was a great example of the reformer role and continued to advocate for marginalized communities.

Edward, a freshman track-and-field athlete and scholar, assumed leadership and advocacy roles through campus involvement and leadership. He was an active member of the Black Student Union and the Gay/Straight Alliance organizations on his campus, creating intersecting spaces that have not historically connected by representing his Black, queer, college athlete activist identity. Keenly aware of how his identities intersect, he walked boldly into these marginalized spaces on campus striving to utilize his platforms to dismantle oppression and racism on campus. Moreover, Edward continues to unapologetically accept the call to activism:

"I've always used my athletics as a platform to speak up for what I believe in. The moment I decided to step into that world, I knew I was never going to be able to step out. Once you're an activist, once you decide to be an activist for something, for something that you believe in, people are always going to remember that."

The reformer role can take on many faces, depending on who is called to engage in their activism that way. Because I have worked, researched, and mentored diverse individuals, I have seen reformers operate in the most fascinating avenues to make change. A friend of mine, Charlotte, is one of the best community activists I have known. She loves her city, her husband, and her two awesome children. Any time her city is hosting an event, especially if it centers marginalized communities, I can count on running into Charlotte there with the biggest smile on her face.

Recently, because of her positionality and recognition in her city, she proposed her city recognize Kwanzaa as a citywide holiday as well as sponsor a city Kwanzaa event, where she invited me to speak about the Kwanzaa principle of Kujichagulia, also known as Self-Determination. She single-handedly coordinated this incredible event that was not only educational to those who were not familiar with Kwanzaa, but the event also created such a space of pride and community in the city.

Charlotte has been a longtime leader in her children's Parent-Teacher Association (PTA), having managed or led community events like the children's arts festivals and her daughter's Girl Scouts initiatives, as well as serving as a volunteer coordinator on many city initiatives. Her goal is to be an integral part to reform and advocate for ensuring equity and opportunity for every family in her city. She is an incredible example of a reformer in her community.

My role as a faculty member and administrator allows me to engage in the reformer role in activism. In addition to serving as faculty, I also hold a great number of administrative responsibilities as a member of the leadership team in my program. As a reformer, I use my voice to reform, rewrite, and advocate for the change or dismantling of outdated and archaic policies and procedures, as well as advocate for textbooks of BIPOC and LGBTQIA authors in my program, among many other tasks.

Recently, I served as a lead committee member of the Black Faculty, and Staff Association to create an undergraduate Black studies major at our university. We knew that the decision-makers in charge of green-lighting this major did not want to be on the wrong side of history by denying a Black studies major on our campus, and they gave us full support to move ahead with the process. As an alum of the university, I knew this major had been overdue for decades. Especially in the current climate of the nation, our group capitalized on the urgency to provide specific and intentional safe and academic spaces for our Black students on campus.

I was a part of teaching and creating curriculum and courses such as The Black Experience in the United States, Black Economics, and Black Campus and Community Activism. I was so honored to be a part of that movement toward providing these avenues of exploration, learning, and growth that lead to a path of equity and social justice for our Black students. In this reformer role, I continue to utilize my positionality as a scholar activist, faculty member, and administrator to challenge systems within the university that are equitable for all students, but particularly marginalized, minoritized, and oppressed students, and I encourage reformers to continue to strive toward this as well.

Now that you have learned about the agitator and reformer role, perhaps these two do not exactly fit where you feel your natural wiring may align and you are wondering what other roles there are. Is there a role in activism where you can operate to educate certain groups and the general public? You just may be called to be a change agent.

Change Agents

Activism originates from embodying a mindset that doesn't settle for the status quo and doesn't condone the approach of "that's how things have always been," which is simply unacceptable. This activism mindset comes from a deep recognition of injustices and a deeply held feeling that doing nothing would be intolerable. Change agents are those who are called to not only embody this mindset, but desire to educate diverse populations on the importance of that mindset and how to take action in that mindset. Change agents work to educate, organize, and involve the general public to actively oppose present policies and seek positive, constructive solutions. The change agent approaches activism with clarity and intentionality by placing importance on the word *active* and examining the history of oppressed groups and their activism. Considering the tools that worked well and learning from what did not work, change agents take action to make change happen by educating, organizing, and mobilizing.

Bailey, a senior rhetoric major and track athlete explicated not just the action of a change agent, but the meta-cognition and thought process that occurs when engaging in activism:

> *"Activism is not just that very active, very physical thing. It's more of a mindset than anything, because every day you have to think about what you're going through and how you should go against it. It's just changing your thinking and rearranging your thinking, and helping others to rearrange theirs or operate on their modes of thinking. Activism is a way of life. Specifically, an activist is an individual who understands and sees disparities and acts to work against them in the political, social, economic, spiritual, and every type of factor that makes a human and affects human interactions."*

Similarly focusing on the word *active*, Kristin, a sophomore soccer player, business major, and women's history minor, shared a similar definition:

> *"An activist, to me, is someone who doesn't just talk the talk, but also walks the walk. Anyone can sit here and say, 'Oh I support Women's Rights, I support Black Rights, I support Gay and Lesbian Rights.' But an activist is the one who actually goes out and does something about it. It is acting upon their words."*

August, a former college athlete and current educator, counselor, and mentor to young Black and Latinx youth, has engaged in the agitator and reformer activist roles before, but thrives while operating in the change agent role. This has been a lifelong calling he has dedicated himself to. He shared one of the ways he engages in the change agent role:

"I think before certain topics became hot-button issues in the larger society, this was still an issue of urgency for me. I am a middle school counselor and have been at schools where the families of color came from lower socioeconomic backgrounds that affected my students, especially the young men who did not have their fathers present. As a Black man who was fortunate enough to have an active father, I know the impact this can have on a young man well into his adulthood. Because of that, it has become my life's work to be an example for young men. I co-founded a mentoring program where we teach, educate, and empower young Black and brown boys and young men. Exposing them to worlds they may have never had the opportunity to explore is one of the main ways that I engage in activism."

> *"We are striving to change the trajectory of their lives by empowering them to use their voice, navigate systems that were not built for them to succeed in, find their calling, and be great examples for their families and the larger community as young men of color."*
>
> —August, former college athlete and current educator, counselor, and mentor

In addition to the mentoring program in his community, as a school counselor, August constantly advocates for equity for students and does this in many ways. He has led restorative justice circles with students, families, and teachers to assist in the rebuilding of relationships and to address conflict within their prospective communities with the hope of encouraging healthier and more constructive solutions. He has seen firsthand that he has provided and assisted students, families, and even fellow educators with identifying healthier communicative and conflict resolution tools that resulted in decreased absences, fewer behavioral issues on and off campus, and lowered suspensions of students in the minoritized and disenfranchised groups he has served. Numerous parents have thanked him for giving their kids spaces during difficult moments in their lives. August's work as a change agent reaches further than the education system; the seeds he's planted will impact the next generation to not just empower themselves, but to empower generations to come.

One of the most incredible students I worked with was Keith, who shared his experiences as a Black cisgender male college athlete activist while also navigating the world with what some may perceive as a disability. Diagnosed in high school with a heart condition that could cause many athletes to quit, as a change agent, Keith advocates for not only his identities as a person of color, but also for those who are athletes with medical or health conditions:

> *"I was diagnosed with high blood pressure and artery stenosis and sickle cell trait. Because the percentage of my blood cell irregularity is super high, I experience a lot of the symptoms as someone with the full-blown disease. So that alone has forced me to make changes in my life, especially in athletics, which has been very difficult. I've been through probably far worse than what I think is impossible. And look at me, I'm still competing at a high level, especially when you're constantly being told that that's not something you can do by doctors, coaches, and peers. And so, I define my activism as being willing to fight for the communities I belong to and fight for the same causes. I feel that not only am I a Black athlete and student leader, but a Black athlete with medical conditions."*

Keith's advocacy to ensure equitable rights and opportunities for athletes with medical conditions is a great example of a change agent. Many athletic departments do not have the proper education or training on how to navigate and support students with salient and especially nonsalient medical conditions and often fail them miserably.

Keith thrives by not only using his voice to share his experiences; he is educating those who work with these athletes to ensure they have an opportunity to follow their dream to play college sports and maintain a healthy lifestyle under their care.

> *Activism originates from embodying a mindset that doesn't settle for the status quo and doesn't condone the approach of "that's how things have always been," which is simply unacceptable.*

As an expecting Dr. Mama (the nickname I gave myself, of course), I entered educational realms on maternity and health that I had adjacent knowledge about before I was pregnant. There is a dynamic group of Black maternal health workers serving as remarkable change agents as Black doulas, midwives, nurses, and caretakers educating expectant mothers, families, and neighboring communities of the realities of the disparities in maternal care, particularly for Black women, and empowering them in the same vein. The historical racism, oppression, and disparities in care for Black mothers has dated back to slavery with the abuse, sterilization, and deaths of Black women at the hands of slaveowners and ill-equipped caretakers. Black moms are three to four times more likely to die from pregnancy or childbirth-related causes than white mothers, and roughly two-thirds of maternal deaths in the U.S. are preventable.[56]

This has created a deep mistrust of the medical field for Black women and arguably for most BIPOC communities. These Black maternal health workers have created incredible spaces, both face-to-face and virtually, to revolutionize the advocacy for Black mothers to be informed and empowered on their rights not only for delivering their children but for equitable postpartum care. Groups, organizations, and events such as *Mama Glow, National Black Doulas Association, Black Breastfeeding Week, Woven Bodies, Dem Black Mamas Podcast,* and *MomsRising.org,* just to name a few, are taking the tools to educate and eradicate inequitable policies and taking action toward Black maternal thriving.

The change agents in the new community have expanded my mind and provided me with crucial tools and resources, allowing me to be confident in delivering and advocating for my baby and my family. The educational resources they have given my family and many families stepping into the realm of parenthood have offered safety, empowerment, and pride. I am grateful for these change agents and life-changers.

> *Depending on the sphere and place, you may be someone who feels deeply called to operate in multiple roles, which is known as the role of a versatile activist.*

Versatile Activists

Look at you! You have engaged in the strengths-based cognitive behavioral approach of *search and construct!* By doing your soul work and identifying within yourself who you are and why you are called now to lean into your activism, and by learning the roles of activism, you are beginning to construct what your role is in this work for freedom and social justice. Reflecting on the roles in this chapter, do you lean into the role of a reformer, working within systems to dismantle, change, or make policies more equitable from within? Are you an agitator, someone who puts issues on society's agenda through dramatic, nonviolent actions that prevent society from ignoring or denying a violation of widely held value? Or do you lean into the role of a change agent, someone who works to educate, organize, and involve the general public to actively oppose present policies and seek positive, constructive solutions? However, depending on the sphere and place, you may be someone who feels deeply called to operate in multiple roles, which is known as the role of a versatile activist.

I want to give a space for those who do not feel deeply compelled to subscribe to any one role of activism because you may thrive in multiple realms as a versatile activist. This may be someone who has access to reforming policies within systems, who is also able to put those systems on notice publicly as an agitator, and who is able to educate multiple spheres in the community as a change agent. This is someone who is engaging in the most versatile roles of activism. Ultimately, this movement calls for action, and if you feel called to walk in all three of these roles at your most powerful self, this is where your influence is crucial to your continued growth as an activist!

As you reflect on these roles of activism, what is your sphere of influence? We all have them; it can be your family, a group of friends, academic or community spaces, or even larger spheres due to social media—you have an influence. Many believe that you have to have hundreds, thousands, or even millions of followers or need to hold a leadership position to hold weight with your voice, but believe it or not, someone is always watching, learning, and waiting to hear you. I invite you to investigate what role or roles fall naturally inside your wiring.

What are you going to do with your sphere(s) of influence in the role(s) you embody?

_____

_____

_____

_____

What are the top five to eight strengths you bring to the table when you have either attempted to engage in activism and advocacy or desired to?

_____

_____

_____

_____

What was your thought process and approach to that?

_____

_____

_____

_____

What actions and behaviors came naturally to you?

_____

_____

_____

_____

In times of conflict, what strengths did you incorporate during those incidences?

_____

_____

_____

_____

> *As you identify what you are naturally wired to do, your confidence will build moving forward as you are finding your seat at the table—and dismantling the rules at the table at the same time.*

CHAPTER SIX

Choose Your Vehicles

*"Power is the ability to define phenomena and to
make these phenomena act in a desired manner."*
—Huey P. Newton

As activists, we reside in an ecosystem with various vehicles to advocate for ourselves, our communities, and the issues we are passionate about. Because of the leadership, divergent tactics, and forms of resistance utilized throughout history, from the likes of the Civil Rights Movement, Black Campus Movement, and the Black Panther Party, activists of today have a slew of vehicles to adopt, engage in, and build upon to create awareness and fight for change. Furthermore, individuals are experiencing a shift in consciousness or awareness and a desire to know where they are called to the fight for social justice.

Moeschberger et al.[57] identified four factors that influence individuals or groups to care about social justice, and the critical role of awareness in moving toward social justice:

(a) Contact with a reality of oppression and/or one group's abusing power held over another group

(b) Increasing awareness, formulating an efficient avenue to create change, and understanding the role of oneself in relation to this change

(c) Developing a deeper understanding of the historical and social contexts related to the situation

(d) Engaging and participating in the process of change

Have you experienced any of these factors in your growth and development in your consciousness that are leading you toward engaging in activism?

_____

_____

_____

_____

Because of the reality of the oppressive structures in every realm of society, activists have diverged from the status quo to engage in a variety of actions to demand change, from lunch counter sit-ins to conferences and coalitions, from protests and occupying spaces to community collaborations, all the while utilizing media and connections with civil rights activists and college athletes.[58] Throughout my journey working with Black College Athlete Activists (BCAAs), student activists, and members of the community, as well as on my own path engaging in multiple vehicles of advocacy and activism, I'd like to share with you some possible vehicles you can utilize in your various roles and callings.

Originated in studying Black athlete activists, Cooper and associates[59] created a typology that describes five categories of activist actions as a lens in understanding the diverse realms of how activism has been actualized by Black and African American athletes. These categories are symbolic, scholarly, grassroots, sports-based, and economic vehicles of activism. For the purpose of the AGM, I will expound on three of those vehicles:

(a) Public display or symbolic

(b) Scholarly

(c) Grassroots

My goal is that the breakdown of these overarching vehicles will provide resources, guidance, and a starting point on the multitude of ways you can operationalize your activism.

Public Display/Symbolic Activism

Symbolic activism is defined as exhibiting deliberate actions designed to draw attention to social injustices and inspire positive changes in political, educational, economic, and social sectors.[60] This is the most common perception of what activism and advocacy solely looks like and is perhaps the most mainstream vehicle utilized throughout history to bring about awareness of various causes. Public display, or symbolic, activism is commonly exhibited through protests, marches, walks for causes, kneeling, or some public act done individually or in a group setting.

Throughout history there have been a multitude of public displays or symbolic activism as vehicles to bring about awareness of injustices toward Black, Indigenous, and People of Color (BIPOC) as well as the LGBTQIA population. On February 1, 1960, four students from North Carolina A&T State University, Ezell Blair, Jr., Joseph McNeil, Franklin McCain, and David Richmond, were frustrated with the unjust treatment at establishments and wanted to do something about it. They occupied a "whites-only" lunch counter at a Woolworth's store in Greensboro, NC.[61] Although the restaurant refused to serve these students, the four stayed firm in their seats until the establishment closed for the day.

Returning the next day, and joined by two more classmates, William Smith and Clarence Henderson, the students were again refused service, yet they did not relinquish their seats. These students endured harassment from white patrons and naysayers, mental and physical abuse about their inferior status, and refusal to be acknowledged as patrons or human beings.

> *They were spat on, had drinks thrown on their heads and faces, and endured overall violence against their unarmed bodies; nonetheless, they persisted.*

Within five days of the initial lunch counter sit-in, hundreds of sit-ins were organized, and every day for six months, Black students returned to the lunch counter. Over time, their numbers swelled.[62] Media outlets reported the

"Greensboro Four"[63] sit-ins and other sit-ins that followed. These sit-ins were believed to have launched the most pivotal period of student activism, leading to a blueprint of how activism is demonstrated today.[64]

An epitome of engaging and participating in the process of change through the symbolic and public displays of activism was the five-month-long protest initiated by the Black Student Union (BSU) at San Francisco State in 1968. Greatly influenced by the Civil Rights Movement and the involvement and relationships many student activists had with the Black Panther Party, Black student activists engaged in revolutionary activity.[65]

Students at San Francisco State University (SFSU), a Dominantly White Institution (DWI), pushed for equity in curriculum change; admissions increases in students of color in the California State University system that was overwhelmingly filtering Black students to the junior college rather than the state university; the creation of a Black Studies department; and overall equity for Black students, staff, and faculty.[66]

After SFSU's administration showed slow progress in the BSU's demands for equity for 2 years, the BSU and a group of student leaders of color formed the Third World Liberation Front in the fall of 1968, which included the BSU, the Latin American Student Organization, the Filipino American Student Organization, and the Mexican American Student Organization. After negotiations with the Third World Liberation Front and members of the faculty, the president and other university administrators at SFSU agreed to meet the demands of the students.[67] The strike at SFSU was a watershed moment in history.

The longest student-led campus strike in U.S. history laid the groundwork for the establishment of the SFSU College of Ethnic Studies that would later expand to Chicano, Native American, and Asian American programs on their campus and throughout the country.[68] The support student activists received from the neighborhoods, faculty, staff, and multiple communities of disenfranchised groups was the first in the history of student-led protests. The strike at SFSU in 1968 continues to be the blueprint for student-led strikes in the larger scope of activism.[69]

Black activism researchers have posited that 1968 was the pinnacle of the Black and African American athlete engagement in activism, particularly because of protests.[70] This historic moment is commonly referred to as the Black Campus Movement (BCM).

The 1968 Olympics set the stage for the most recognized public demonstration of symbolic activism.

Two San Jose State University athletes, gold medalist Tommie Smith and bronze medalist John Carlos, wore black leather gloves, symbolically raised their fists in the air, lowered their heads, and stood barefoot on the podium as the national anthem was played.[71] Both athletes utilized the international platform as a public protest to spread awareness of injustices and inequalities in the Black community and other oppressed communities back home. The image of their fists in the air was a powerful symbol of power, resistance, and pride and continues to be a staple of Black power in present-day resistance movements.[72]

Black campus activists and the BCM disturbed more than 150 campuses during the 1967–68 academic year, with the majority of these disturbances occurring after the assassination of Martin Luther King, Jr.[73] There were 250 more protests from 1968 to 1969, and more than 150 incidents the following year.[74] The role of Black student movements in U.S. higher education from the mid-1960s to the early 1970s was instrumental in causing the implementation of new racial policies. The BCM has utilized, and continues to utilize, strategies and tactics that have frustrated and defeated oppositional structures.[75]

An example of a modern-day collective effort between student activists and athlete activists took center stage in 2015 when members of the University of Missouri football team stood in solidarity with Concerned Student 1950, a group of student activists, to protest the multiple racialized incidents on campus.[76] The Black football players protested playing in their upcoming nationally televised game unless the president and chancellor of the university resigned. Their individual efforts to engage in collective tactics of boycotting their game resulted in the resignation of both administrators that, arguably, sparked the college athlete activist movement of the 21st century.[77]

Relatedly, perhaps the most polarizing and controversial athlete activist of the 21st century so far is Colin Kaepernick, for his simple yet courageous act during the 2016 football season of kneeling during the national anthem.[78] Kaepernick utilized the act of kneeling to protest against social injustice, especially the deaths of African Americans at the hands of police, as well as the unfair treatment and lack of support of veterans.[79]

> *Risking his career, notoriety, and athlete status, Kaepernick was a pivotal figure in the 21st century to embody symbolic activism to call for social justice.*

One fist in the air, kneeling, and sporting his throwback Afro, Kaepernick became the face of the Black athlete resistance in the 21st century. Empowering a generation while paying homage to the Black athlete activists who paved the way, Kaepernick continues to be a polarizing figure of resistance as well as the face of isolation, a cost with which the BCAAs in my study can identify.

Furthermore, although his quarterback statistics are on par with quarterbacks currently in the NFL, Kaepernick has not been asked to play on an NFL roster since 2016. Kaepernick took a calculated risk of utilizing his positionality as a Black athlete to change the trajectory and conversation of race, sports, and politics, actions for which many participants thanked him.

Dr. Martin Luther King, Jr., declared this illustration of public displays or symbolic activism in his speech on March 14, 1968, proclaiming that protests are the language of the unheard.[80] These words continue to galvanize and ignite the Black community as protests and other forms of public displays of activism reemerge in the present day.

In my research over the past few years, I have witnessed some incredible activists utilize public and symbolic displays of activism as a vehicle to lean into their activist identity. Logan, a senior student leader, volleyball player, history major, and community activist reflected on the moment when her activism reached a new level of expression on her campus through her athlete identity by kneeling during the national anthem:

> *"I was just so angry with everything that was going on in the news…. I just started by not putting my hand over my heart because I didn't want to be too dramatic, but then also I couldn't stand there and honor a flag and honor a country that's not honoring me…. I said to myself, I don't know how to help. I don't know what I can do from this standpoint except take a knee. I took a knee, and then ever since then, I just kept doing it. That is not who I am anymore. I can't go back."*

Consequently, when Logan began exercising her activism by kneeling at her volleyball games during the national anthem, other Black athletes, Black students, allies, and accomplices began to exercise their activism and show their solidarity. Her internal trigger to the police brutality taking place in the nation called her to display her activism publicly, bringing awareness to such injustices.

Kristin, a sophomore student leader, activist, and business major participated in the historic 2017 Women's March, the largest single-day protest in U.S. history. The impetus of the Women's March in 2017 was to vehemently oppose the election of the 45th President of the United States and the divisive hate-mongering his administration stood on, and quite frankly throughout his entire disastrous one term.

Initially, the goal of the march that since became an annual event was to advocate for legislation and policies regarding human rights and other issues, including women's rights, immigration reform, healthcare reform, reproductive rights, the environment, LGBTQIA rights, racial equality, freedom of religion, workers' rights, and tolerance. Kristin proudly marched and stood in solidarity with women of color, allies, and accomplices and helped organize and participate in multiple Black Lives Matter marches in collaboration with her Black Student Union and other student organizations on her campus.

Lastly, I would be remiss not to mention a beautiful public display and symbolic form of activism that was recently created as a result of the climate of the nation. It began when the Mayor of Washington, D.C., Muriel Bowser, commissioned a BLACK LIVES MATTER mural, painted in huge yellow letters, down the middle of 16th Street NW, the street that runs right up to the North Lawn of the White House. This image is so large that you can see it from outer space—yes, I said outer space. The mural was spotted after an update from Apple maps in a satellite view of the street where the words were painted. The bold message in Washington, D.C., incited other cities to follow suit, where similar murals appeared in Raleigh, NC, Sacramento, CA, and Oakland, CA, each larger than life and on downtown and high-traffic streets. Three words that carry such meaning in this moment and illustrate the simple, yet poignant demonstration of the symbolic or public display of activism.

Questions to explore if public display/symbolic activism is a vehicle of activism you would like to utilize:

Do you greatly value the usage of symbolism in your activism? If so, what ways have you incorporated or plan to incorporate symbols in public display/symbolic activism (e.g., murals, signs, wearing a cause)?

_____

_____

_____

_____

At times of opportunities to engage in protests, marches, or demonstrations, did those moments fuel you and invigorate you to continue to engage in such vehicles of activism? If so, describe how you felt during those moments.

_____

_____

_____

_____

In previous times of injustices, did you have the tendency to utilize public platforms to bring awareness to them? What were those outcomes?

_____

_____

_____

_____

When you think about activist ancestors from the past or present whom you admire, what were their most common vehicles of choice? If they utilized public display/symbolic activism, explore characteristics you admire about their utilization of that vehicle of activism.

_____

_____

_____

_____

Scholarly Activism

Scholarly activism uses scholarship and acquisition of knowledge to disrupt the notion that education and the furthering of information is property held solely for white individuals. Scholarly activism is the practice of contributing to the breaking of barriers and boundaries in the academic or intellectual sphere. Freire[81] stated that education is a tool that can be used to liberate and promote growth, but it has also been used within this country to maintain a racial status quo.

> *If you desire to engage in scholarly activism, will you be a part of breaking barriers and pushing boundaries, or will you maintain the status quo of inequity? You have the pen, and you are the architect.*

Scholarly activism has been demonstrated in dissertations, theses, academic majors, presentations, books, chapters, and teaching courses. Those are more "traditional" realms of scholarly activism; however, the expanding and growing avenues in which scholarly activism can be displayed are endless. Each new generation of activists creates new and divergent ways to change the landscape of scholarly activism and advocacy. Individuals and groups are blogging, podcasting, and engaging on social media and television about topics and issues of social injustice and inequalities, avenues that were nonexistent decades prior.

Cooper et al.[82] called this present-day generation of activism "securing and transferring power via economic and technological capital." Activism in the 21st century has been connected to strategic use of various types of technology and social media as tools for disruption, information dissemination, organization, and empowerment.[83] For instance, a study conducted by Bailard in 2012 examined the influences of the Internet on the motivation of individuals to organize and effect political change, specifically, surrounding the 2010 election in Tanzania. The author found one-third of participants specifically sought information about the election online, and nearly two-thirds reported mostly using the Internet to gather news and information, assuaging doubts regarding individuals' desire to seek information about their own governments while online.[84]

This study speaks directly to how social media today has been and continues to be a beacon of information and resources not only to urge individuals to vote for upcoming elections, but to learn about local propositions that affect our neighborhoods, cities, districts, and states from multiple political and scholarly activists providing educational spaces on social media. As definitions of individual acts of activism vary, the avenue by which individuals display their activism continues to diversify as well.

The student leaders and athlete activists I worked with over the years have engaged in scholarly activism through their academic majors and what they were striving to do with their degrees after they graduated. The athlete activists represented diverse majors as follows:

- Logan: As a political science major, she got accepted to law school to be a civil rights attorney and has begun her graduate school journey.

- Keith: Double majoring in history and African American studies, he has the goal of broadening his understanding of the systems of oppression that have been developed over time against his community to engage in community leadership.

- Kristin: A business major minoring in African American studies, she strives to further her knowledge in career development opportunities for Black women breaking barriers in business.

- Owen: Majoring in geography and psychology, he is interested in environmental activism, particularly as it affects communities of color.

- Bailey: As a rhetoric major, she engaged in scholarly activism by writing her thesis on Black women in the academy, and desires to earn her doctorate soon.

- Darren: A psychology major who will be starting graduate school in sport management, he plans to advocate for the improvement of preparing athletes for life after sports in their chosen majors.

- Alexandria: She engages in scholarly activism as a political science major by continuing to educate herself as well as others on voting and empowering her communities.

- Austin: A political science major with an African studies minor, he plans to pursue graduate school to further his education and knowledge on the historical injustices that have plagued BIPOC.

> *Whether you are engaging in scholarly activism to communicate to certain realms or communities with a specific goal of confronting existing power relations, or to speak the truth directly to the people in your communities, you are speaking truth to power.*

With the knowledge you have and continue to acquire as a scholarly activist, not only are you continuing to educate and empower yourself, you are igniting changes on your campus and in your community to empower the next generation of activists. Ultimately, your voice matters! Continue to infiltrate knowledge spaces as well as create avenues of your own.

Questions to explore if scholarly activism is a vehicle of activism you would like to utilize:

Are you in a position or place where you can focus on activism and advocacy in your current educational setting (i.e., training and certificate programs, community education, undergraduate, academic majors, graduate or doctoral programs, etc.)? If so, what is your focus?

_____

_____

_____

_____

Are there educational programs or settings of interest where you would like to further your knowledge of activism and advocacy? If so, what are they?

_____

_____

_____

_____

What topics or issues can you pursue to increase your knowledge of activism and advocacy? Where can you obtain this knowledge (i.e., books, webinars, mentors, credible social media outlets, and so forth)?

_____

_____

_____

_____

Grassroots Activism

Simply put, grassroots activism is created from the ground up, where a group of people who feel strongly enough about an issue actively campaign to make a difference. Grassroots activism can originate from the local level to affect change at the local, regional, national, or international level. Grassroots activism has no boundary, as it can be demonstrated through programs, campaigns, causes, organizations, businesses, and positions toward a cause, issue, or topic you are passionate about.

The heinous injustices plaguing the Black and African American community in the 1960s ignited the Black community to continue to organize and agitate against white supremacist structures on both college campuses and in society. This in turn was the impetus for the formation of one of the most prolific grassroots organizations in history, the Black Panther Party (BPP), which was originally called the Black Panther Party for Self-Defense. As described in Chapter 1, the BPP was originally created in 1966 in Oakland, CA.

Since Huey P. Newton and Bobby Seale were students at Merritt College, they were in close company with other Black students who were also deeply affected by what they saw as the failure of the Civil Rights Movement to achieve substantive progress. Newton and Seale, building on their established connections with other Black power organizations, founded the Black Panther Party for Self-Defense, which grew to become the most powerful and far-reaching Black movement in history.[85]

The BPP stood in the gap to protect the Black community from police brutality and community violence. It successfully launched neighborhood patrols and provided much-needed support for improving education outcomes, addressing legal concerns, and responding to transportation inequities. Its Free Breakfast for Children Program was active in every major American city with a BPP presence.[86]

Many prominent names in activism were involved in the BPP, including Eldridge and Kathleen Cleaver, Angela Davis, Fred Hampton, and Stokely Carmichael.[87] The ten-point program developed by the BPP outlined the organizers' principal stance, with demands rooted in equality and justice. The BPP had chapters in several major American cities and paved the way for other movements like the Gay Rights Movement, the Women's Movement, the Chicano Studies Movement, and the Environmental Movement, among others.[88] College students have been at the forefront of each of these grassroots movements.[89]

> *The Black Panther Party is a beautiful illustration of what manifests when the climate creates a platform out of necessity, the epitome of grassroots activism.*

Other pivotal examples of grassroots activism were the creation of conferences and coalitions formed by Black student activists that intertwined with the Civil Rights Movement, known as the Black Campus Movement (BCM). These spaces were monumental for Black students to develop their movement ideology, methodology, and force.[90]

These conferences, coalitions, and groups were breeding grounds to cultivate their consciousness of Black power that enhanced their self-worth, self-determination, and standing in solidarity of the power they held to make their institutions of learning a better place for all.

In the fall of 1964, Columbia and Barnard students established the Student Afro-American Society (SAS) for students to discuss African American problems with hopes of solutions and to create future leaders. From May 1 to May 4, 1964, the Afro-American Student Movement launched the Afro-American Student Conference on Black Nationalism at Fisk University, essentially the "ideological catalyst that eventually shifted the Civil Rights Movement to Black power."[91]

During the BCM, multitudes of Black Student Unions (BSUs) were formed. In fact, many BSUs were created from the framework in which the Black Panther Party (BPP) was formed. Modeling the BPP's ten-point program, the BSU at the University of Washington also developed a ten-point program and some organizations changed their position titles from president to prime minister just as the BPP named their officers.

Examining the phenomenon of activism taking place 50 years after the Civil Rights Movement, according to the Pew Research Center,[92] a majority of Americans (65%) continue to say there are very strong or strong conflicts between Blacks and whites in the United States. Furthermore, the deaths of young, unarmed Black men and boys by white law enforcement at the turn of the 21st century is both heartbreaking and predictable, lending truth to those conflicts between Blacks and whites.

Recently, because of media attention, America has been privy to the lynching of Black bodies. Moreover, the nonsanctioned actions of the officers operationalize the disregard for Black bodies, with the overwhelming majority of police shooting cases ultimately determined to be justified homicides.[93]

The actions and nonsanctions prove that racism is salient and Black bodies continue to be exterminated.[94] Coates[95] posited that the "police departments of your country have been endowed with the authority to destroy your body," and "the destroyers will rarely be held accountable. Mostly, they will receive pensions."

To a majority of Black America, the police reflect white supremacy in "all of its will and fear."[96] This is a devastating reality most of society refuses to recognize.[97] Because of this, scholars have noticed the existence of a specific type of social movement called "new emotional movements," which, as mentioned earlier, are often born in response to highly publicized violent events or are, more broadly, a direct reaction to a "suddenly imposed grievance."[98]

Other scholars have referred to these new types of movements as "pain and loss activism,"[99] "focusing event protests,"[100] protest resulting from "moral shocks,"[101] or "social responsibility movements."[102] The Black Lives Matter (BLM) movement is a perfect example of this type of movement. It was ignited by the lynching of unarmed Black citizens by police and armed civilians.[103] The BLM movement began as a Black-centered awareness-raising project designed to build community cohesion and launch a movement for justice. It has since grown exponentially into a vast network of chapters led by members with a clear mission to strengthen local power bases and challenge the threat of state and vigilante violence against the members of Black communities.[104]

Similarly, a common example of grassroots activism has been utilized through the usage of campaigns.[105] A campaign is composed of multiple tactics of activism where a group of tactics are ventured together. Although sometimes tactics are undertaken in isolation, when a series of tactics are executed to achieve the same goal, the activism effort is called a campaign. Furthermore, Keck and Sikkink[106] explicated campaigns as strategically linked activities where individuals in a network develop explicit roles toward a common goal, generally against a common target.

A number of campaigns or grassroots organizations sprouted during the Civil Rights Movement: the Congress of Racial Equality (CORE), the National Association for the Advancement of Colored People (NAACP), and Southern Christian Leadership Conference (SCLC). These were fundamental in the sustainability of the Civil Rights Movement and the Black Campus Movement (BCM).[107] From the early 1960s to the present day, these groups have been integral to the role of student activism on campuses organizing for their civil rights.[108]

Colin Kaepernick's Know Your Rights Campaign (KYRC) was born as the pinnacle of love and liberation for Black and brown communities to know their rights when facing situations when engaging with law enforcement. The campaign was a labor of love that foreshadowed poignant words he said during the press conference in August 2016, after the first time he knelt during the national anthem.

Among a multitude of social justice issues, Kaepernick spoke of police brutality gravely affecting the Black and brown communities. Utilizing his platform as the most polarizing athlete activist of the time, Kaepernick and his partner, Nessa, centering the issues of systemic anti-Blackness and police terrorism, created the KYRC, a traveling youth-empowerment initiative designed to serve as a home base and safe space for Black youth ages 12–18.

KYRC's primary goal is to give participants legal knowledge for navigating all-too-common violent encounters with police officers through education and self-empowerment, to create the next generation of change leaders. Adopting the formula of the Black Panther Party's ten-point program, KYRC is curated by ten fundamental human rights; the principles represent the types of affirmations and protections that should be afforded to and enjoyed by Black people globally. KYRC participants learn, recite, and carry these principles with them well after leaving the camp:

> *You have the right to be Free*
>
> *You have the right to be Healthy*
>
> *You have the right to be Brilliant*
>
> *You have the right to be Safe*
>
> *You have the right to be Loved*
>
> *You have the right to be Courageous*
>
> *You have the right to be Alive*
>
> *You have the right to be Trusted*
>
> *You have the right to be Educated*
>
> *You have the right to Know Your Rights*

Using grassroots activism with love at the root of all he does, Colin Kaepernick's legacy will last for many generations to come.

During my time working with athletes and student leaders, many identified and actualized their activism by engaging in grassroots activism. They created diversified spaces for Black athletes and students at their prospective institutions by identifying a need for their community and taking action. Seniors Bailey and Owen were eager to leave a legacy to empower the Black athletes they would be leaving behind after graduation.

Consequently, January 2017 provided an opportunity that would catapult them into that grassroots activism leadership role. They were three of the four chosen scholar athletes to attend the third annual Black Student Athlete Summit at the University of Texas in Austin. The summit, which launched in 2015, offers workshops, panels, and sessions to discuss racism, stereotypes, and the overall experiences of Black college athletes.

Bailey's experience at the Black Student Athlete Summit was transformational as she connected with other Black college athletes who were also passionate about bringing change and creating a space for fellow athletes at their institution:

> *"The athletes I met there; we experienced a lot of the same issues on our campuses. It was so empowering because sometimes you can't speak to other people about the issues that you have because they don't understand it. Meeting other athletes from all over the country was such an important experience; it was community. Community empowers me because it's strength in numbers. It's understanding in a space. When you're in a space where you can understand and talk with people who have the same feelings, who also have arguments for different ways to go about things, it becomes a really eye-opening experience, in realizing these people have these other worlds and experiences behind them. I wanted to create that back at my school."*

Owen, a geography and psychology major and football player, also reflected on this life-changing experience at the summit, especially where the students and speakers addressed what it's like being a Black athlete in the age of Black Lives Matter. He wanted to create a space at his institution for Black athlete activists to also feel empowered:

> *"The summit just made me feel empowered. It made me feel like I need to be like a lighthouse to the other Black athletes. I could bring more people in, being a lighthouse to everybody in the storm. I feel like our community's in the storm right now. So, creating this group would be building lighthouses."*

Another group of incredible athletes not only formed a space of activism and advocacy for themselves on their campus, but have expanded it on the national level.

I had the pleasure of meeting a dynamic former college athlete and current activist, Mikaela, during one of my biweekly National Collegiate Athlete Activism Call meetings to support current athlete activists in navigating their collegiate careers as well as advocating for themselves, particularly in the COVID-19 era.

Mikaela, a former four-year track-and-field athlete, also attended the Black Student Athlete Summit in Texas a few years ago. She was so moved by the collective space of Blackness and empowerment that she felt compelled to co-found the Coalition for African Diaspora Student-Athletes (CADSA) on her campus in 2017.

Still going strong, CADSA has collaborated with other student-led grassroots organizations, such as College Athletes for No More Names, College Athletes Unity, Athletes Igniting Action, and Athletes for Change, as they all seek to serve college athletes who face more risks of financial stress and mental health issues, as well as more experiences of insufficient access to professional development, low graduation rates, and lack of mentorship than any other group on campus.[109]

Now an alum and the Expansion Director, she and her colleagues have expanded CADSA to a national level to "unite those who identify as such across our campus and throughout the country. With our collective voice, we call out and combat the anti-Black racism that student-athletes within the Diaspora face."

An idea that was birthed from the need of additional support for Black athletes on her campus, grassroots activism was in full effect as Mikaela and company have built and continue to build a legacy of empowerment and advocacy where Black college athletes on every campus are welcomed, supported, and heard.

As a doctoral student a few years back, in my cohort, I was one of only three Black students out of fifteen. Before my cohort, there were one or two Black Ph.D. students in the program overall. However, there were a few more Black students on the Ed.D. side of our higher education department. Because of scheduling and the different academic tracks the Ph.D. and Ed.D. students were on, we did not have many opportunities to organically spend time with one another.

> *I quickly realized the unique experience it was to be a Black doctoral student at a predominantly white, faith-based institution studying issues on race, social justice, and inequity, and the importance of creating a safe space to develop as a scholar activist.*

Feeling a sense of onlyness and a desire to create an unapologetic Black academic space, I desired to create an organization that was curated for such an experience. I received support from my program chair and was provided resources and contacts in order to legitimize the organization I founded called the Black Doctoral Student Association. We hosted lunches and study nights, created an online identity where we connected with alums of our programs, served as representatives on the doctoral advisory board, and created "Blackademic" shirts that still turn heads when we wear them on our various campuses. I served as the founding president for two years until I earned my Ph.D., and I am so proud of my successors who have carried the baton, collaborating with other Black doctoral students on campus to create an expansive, supportive space for Black students.

Like the Know Your Rights Campaign, Black Lives Matter, the Black Panther Party, the Civil Rights Movement, and so many other examples in this chapter, justice and equality for all is the foundation. The individual is the fundamental unit of activism; an individual can either take action alone or collectively.[110] All these qualify as grassroots vehicles of activism. The beauty of grassroots activism is that if there is a desire burning inside of you to organize, create, or revamp because there isn't an existing program or organization that serves your passion, this is where you shine.

> *Necessity is the mother of invention, the foundation of grassroots activism.*

Questions to explore if grassroots activism is a vehicle of activism you would like to utilize:

Reflect on your ecosystem (friends, family, local and social media community, etc.). Can you identify opportunities where you desire to build campaigns, organizations, or programs?

_____

_____

_____

_____

Are there topics or issues you have passion about that you want to share or build upon? If so, what are they? The time is now! Your voice and experience matters!

_____

_____

_____

_____

If you received a grant or funding for the cause of activism, what would you do with that funding? Would you create something from the grassroots level? If so, what comes to mind?

_____

_____

_____

_____

As participants in my studies shared their personal experiences and vehicles of activism, some commonalities emerged, such as obtaining an internal consciousness and awareness of inequality, making mindful decisions in standing up against oppression, and actively using their voices to create awareness to ultimately make change. Furthermore, the activists I worked with utilized various vehicles of activism via their platforms to pursue social justice and, as their desires to speak truth were ignited, their activism manifested in diverse methods. I hope these examples of activism vehicles provide insight, empowerment, and road maps toward doing your own form of liberation.

CHAPTER SEVEN

Find Your People

"Without community, there is no liberation."
—Audre Geraldine Lorde

Although the previous pillars are of great importance to grow and develop your advocacy and activism, finding your people is critical to sustaining your motivation to step into spaces full of resistance. This is why finding like-minded individuals who see your potential, passion, and promise is imperative. Your tribe and community can be family, peers, mentors, or individuals who belong to causes and groups you identify with; literary communities; and intellectual support communities. Ultimately, you cannot walk this journey alone, and having people who see and empower you is how you will survive and thrive.

Family as Your Community of Support

In some instances, your people and your community can originate from those who raised you, your family. Some of the folks in my studies shared that they learned to be activists from the legacy of the generations of activism that their parents and family bestowed upon them. This shared familial vision is defined by Vargas[111] as family activism. This occurs when families engage in activism that shares similar vision and commitment and becomes a force to influence larger circles of community to initiate campaigns, marches, organizations, and projects to further social justice.

In Vargas' *Five Principles to Guide Family Activism*, the majority of the study participants' narratives embodied two of the five principles seamlessly: (a) "you and your family model the change you desire in the world," and (b) "families who encourage vision and transformation will advance social transformation through

71

vision and personal change."[112] My work with the student and community activists supports previous findings on family that stress the importance of strong support and encouragement from family and extended family members as foundational to a mindset of activism and social justice.[113]

Similarly, Riffer[114] examined the sources of students' political attitudes and found parents had a strong impact on participants' political socialization. Additionally, Assibey and Mensah[115] found both siblings and parents served as primary influences on participants. Supporting previous research, many participants expressed the importance of being a role model for their family and community as they strive to advocate for themselves and their communities.

Participants in my studies consistently shared that their family has been committed to social justice and actively taking leadership roles in their community for generations, lending an important contributing factor to their engagement in activism. In fact, for some participants, family was and is a huge piece of their identity, serving as an individual antecedent to activism.

Consequently, for activists born from a lineage of activism, engaging in social justice is a family norm. For example, Logan recalled the role her family played in her activism:

> *"My upbringing—it is as if I feel like I was raised just to be confident and not really care about what other people think, and do what I need to do. I feel like that helped when it came down to first kneeling and knowing that people were watching me."*

Because of the support and empowerment of his family, Austin embodies an awareness of his positionality and platform. This awareness was developed with his personal accountability along with the support and vision of his family and support system:

> *"I'm close with my family. My parents were always like, 'Wherever you go, whatever you see, put your mind to it, you do it.' So, definitely,*

my parents and brother, and my immediate family, have always been
supportive in my activism."

Darren, a senior football captain and psychology major, has a foundation of pursuing justice because his family is rooted in the practice of love and the desire to pursue righteousness. He undoubtedly conducts himself in a manner that embodies that foundation. He reflected on his support, especially by his family:

> *"My parents are really the ones that have been there helping and guiding*
> *me toward being who I am right now in terms of activism and things of*
> *that nature. I have talks like this with my mom a lot, and sometimes I*
> *have talks like this with my father as well, but it's a lot of the times with*
> *my mom. She watches a lot of political things on TV and stuff, but they*
> *both tell me if there's things I can do to help change what's going on, then*
> *do them."*

There is a close connection between the narratives of the student and community activists in my studies on the power of the family's experience with those of Yosso's[116] Cultural and Community Wealth model, particularly, the familial capital of the model.

Yosso's familial capital centers the importance of the social and personal capital students had in their pre-college environment originating from their family and cultural networks. These resources and capital can hail from myriad avenues, such as cultural knowledge, traditions, counterstories of empowerment, and liberatory behaviors modeled in their homes and community.

Similarly, aligning with the cruciality of recognizing students' cultural and familial wealth, participants in my studies supported this observation as they shared that their earliest influences of activism were drawn from their immediate and extended familial and community networks. Looking closer at the emergent theme of family, it should be noted that Black women in particular have played critical roles as mothers, aunts, and grandmothers in the development of activism consciousness for many participants.

> *This lends truth to the ongoing reality that throughout the history of activism and the struggle for freedom, Black women have been the visionaries, building blocks, hedges of protection, and forces with which to be reckoned.*

A perfect example of this testament is Austin. Although Austin is a product of a two-parent household, he attributes who he is today to the strength, support, and guidance his mother provided him throughout his life, a statement not uncommon to his fellow Black College Athlete Activist (BCAA) counterparts.

Keith also exclaimed that the only validation he needs in his life is his "mama and God, and that's it" as she has been his biggest supporter and sounding board while he cultivated his activist identity. Kristen, a multiracial woman of color, heard stories of her immigrant Asian mother and grandmother as well as her Black grandmother of the struggles, strength, and sacrifices both sides of her family made to fight for equality for both their race and gender, a strength she relies on in her call and dedication to women's rights in her own activism.

Another example is Logan's familial capital, which served as a huge piece of her activist identity. Her mother and aunt participated in marches and community activism and shared those stories with her. Such liberatory practices continue in her life today. Her mother and aunt, although volunteering at the snack bar during her games, would stop and sit as Logan knelt during the national anthem. An unequivocally beautiful illustration of continuous resistance and supportive behavior was embedded and modeled for Logan from her family.

Black Women as the Backbone of the Community of Support

From as early as the abolitionist and anti-slavery movement, Harriet Tubman, known as the Moses of her people after escaping slavery twice, single-handedly emancipated and guided countless numbers of the enslaved to freedom. As the Civil Rights

Movement converged with contemporary activism, Black women have been the unsung heroes of the movement—the backbone to every publicly recognized male representative of the Civil Rights Movement that history chooses to honor. Black women were role models in other ways as well.

One does not always need to be related to people to become a source from which to draw inspiration and courage. For instance, Angela Davis and Kathleen Cleaver were two of the many women revolutionaries in the Civil Rights Movement who emerged in anti-racist activism and women's rights today. Their life stories inspired many activists; their lives inspired me.

Today, the three founders of Black Lives Matter (BLM), Patrisse Khan-Cullors, Alicia Garza, and Opal Tometi, are grounded in centering all Black women's voices and positionality in the current fight against anti-Black state-sanctioned violence and oppression, and in the ongoing fight for the humanity of Blacks all over the world.[117]

Their leadership, organization, and fierce intentionality are the reasons activism, specifically Black activism, has reemerged in society, communities, and especially on college campuses everywhere. Regardless if study participants were male or female gender-identifying, the vision of the three Black female founders of BLM has shaped, formed, and influenced the lens in which activism brings focus into their lives.

Furthermore, Tubman and the unsung freedom fighters of the Civil Rights Movement, along with founders of the womanist movement and BLM, are the quintessential illustrations of the power, determination, and unwavering dedication Black women have to the cause of freedom and justice. This reality held truth in my study as many participants honored the Black women in their lives, and this reality will continue to remain true for decades on end.

The narratives of the student and community activists in my research support previous research that a legacy of family, cultural capital, and activism creates a solid foundation rooted in social justice.

Is your family or extended family a supportive piece of your growth in activism?

_____

_____

_____

_____

_____

A Community of Faith and Spirituality in Activism

Historically, faith has been a source of inspiration to activists,[118] and as some participants expressed, their faith served as a lighthouse on their path to pursue activism. In fact, one of the best-documented examples of this was the 1960s Civil Rights Movement, as many student activists viewed their activism and engagement to be an extension of their faith.[119]

Many of the marches and protests during the Civil Rights Movement commenced with a prayer or song, particularly those in the South led by Dr. Martin Luther King at the 16th Street Baptist Church, and alongside him were students and a gamut of clergymen of various faiths and denominations.[120] As we celebrate the 50th anniversary of the Civil Rights Movement and the Black Campus Movement, some participants attested their faith as an antecedent of their activism, mirroring their activist ancestors.

For many participants, faith and, more specifically, the Christian tradition, had an impact on their activism. Christian faith has historically been a foundation and source of guidance for Black and African Americans, and from the narratives of participants, the influence of faith contributes an individual antecedent of activism.

Because their faith and spirituality have served as a guiding post in every facet of their lives, many participants expressed their individual faith identity as a critical pillar to how their activism was actualized in their quest for social justice.

With God as his foundation in his upbringing, Keith was ready to stand firm for what he believed in as an activist and advocate:

> *"I remember seeing a tweet by one of my friends, "When I go to war, I go to war with God behind me." That really resonated with me because I feel like it was everything I do, despite the challenges, despite any obstacle, or any person that comes against me, I like to remember that I always have God behind me. I personally call on God before I decide to indulge in anything. I think that's super important. And I really don't need anyone else's validation except for one: that would be my mom, and God, really. And those are two."*

Similarly, Owen expressed a strong sense of self, where God continues to guide his actions. He shared that he wears his faith boldly as it framed his experiences as a Black college athlete and reflected on the calling of faith and activism on his life:

> *"I don't see this journey as a sacrifice; I see this journey as a blessing that God has led me on to places I need to be, and because of that I've been able to leave my mark wherever I go."*

> *"This journey God has led me on, I definitely believe I've been called and chosen to do something. I look at history where leaders and activists have made change or stood for a change by sacrificing their interests for the greater good."*
> —Owen, geography and psychology major and football player

Owen's call to engage in activism is both an internal call because of his personal faith and commitment to social justice and an external call to activism because of his heightened awareness of the injustices occurring in his community and in society. Coupled with his family history and his own eagerness to learn about the Civil Rights

Movement, especially in the ways history is repeating itself, Austin approaches his activism with truth and clarity.

Although some participants expressed a Christian identity or used the terms "faith" or God," some students utilized "spirituality as a factor in their activism." Bailey, a female senior track-and-field athlete, shared the role spirituality and her culture played in how she sees the world:

> *"I grew up in a Christian family. However, after continuing to educate myself, I've learned that society needs to put you in this place and keep you from yourself. And sometimes religion can do that, keep you restricted. But my grandparents practiced Yoruba, which is like a Nigerian religion. The household was really focused on spirituality."*

> *"I've always known this sort of peace, and you have to kind of reflect. You have to put out what you want to see back in the world. I relied a lot on the energies and emotions and interpreting the world. So, I would say I fit more into the spiritual, golden rule approach, do unto others as you would like done to you."*
>
> —Bailey, female senior track-and-field athlete

Nonetheless, the student and community activists who expressed an identification of faith or spirituality described that their connection to God or a higher power couldn't allow them to stand passively on the sideline while Black bodies were being devalued. They have committed to utilizing activism as a survival tool because they are simply tired of the unending oppression they experience as it relates to the multiple identities they embody and the community of brothers and sisters in their faith as a part of their support system.

Locating Communities that Speak to Your Passion

As previously mentioned, the BCAAs in my studies who attended the Black Student Athlete Summit in Austin, TX, were empowered to engage in grassroots activism by creating groups and organizations for Black athletes on their campuses, desiring to sustain the electricity that was experienced at the summit. They all came home invigorated to be a part of the resistance while building up the Black community and creating a safe and necessary space.

At a Black Student Athlete Group meeting I attended as I was working on my dissertation, a group of twenty Black college athletes gathered in a safe space to engage in dialogue on the intersectionality of their race, gender, sport, and major at a large, public institution in California.

They shared stories of their personal calls to action, engaging in activism on and off campus, and lack of family and institutional support. They ended the meeting with an opportunity to share and lament on the countless recollections of microaggressions and discrimination on their campus. I asked these scholars about their self-care practices in times of racial and social injustice, and they all simultaneously proclaimed, "These meetings are our self-care!"

Before the creation of the group, the students shared that they sought safe spaces to recharge and rejuvenate but could not find such places. Support groups of this nature are a rare space for activists, and particularly activists of color, to create a space for themselves to discuss the issues of the larger campus culture.

Depending on the campus climate of the institution and community, these types of spaces were historically stifled from being discussed in the open. I am so proud of these dynamic student activists who were keenly aware of finding their community in order to sustain them in their activism.

During my tenure as a higher education practitioner, I've had the pleasure of creating, supporting, and providing opportunities to develop student leadership through workshops, conferences, internships, and other educational and social activities to uplift my students.

One community of support I am incredibly proud to have been a part of was the revitalization of the Black Residential Scholars Living Learning Community and mentoring program at one of my former institutions. Black Residential Scholars (BRS) as a Living Learning Community is known as a high-impact practice in higher education dedicated to supporting scholars through holistic development, leadership, community, and academic success.

This Living Learning Community was even more crucial because curricular and co-curricular programming was curated for the support, education, and empowerment of the African American and Black student community living on campus but ultimately connecting with the larger African American and Black community on campus.

The goal of BRS is to support all African American and Black students and introduce them to campus resources in order for them to successfully navigate the educational experience on campus. I also created a strengths-based mentoring program, where I matched Black faculty, staff, and administration with BRS students to empower them in their academics, social-emotional growth, advocacy, and activism for themselves and their community.

> *Having spaces to safely express all your identities is beneficial to your well-being, especially when these spaces encourage the celebration of your activism, cultures, and identities.*

That is why this tenet is important to establish a connection with people of similar backgrounds, causes, and interests, and to give back to your cultural communities. As you are locating your communities of support to sustain and maintain your energy in times of opposition, explore these facets to find your people:

Who are the like-minded individuals at your school or in your community who share your passion for the causes or topics that engage you in activism?

_____

_____

_____

_____

Are any of these individuals members of your family?

_____

_____

_____

_____

Who are some mentors engaging in and bringing awareness to causes you are interested in? Have you reached out to them to learn more about their passions?

_____

_____

_____

_____

What cause communities are you passionate about that you can locate locally, state-wide or online? (These can include chapter meetings, events, conferences, symposiums, etc.)

_____

_____

_____

_____

How do you search for your literary community and intellectual support communities? (This can include scholar activists who have contributed to resistance in various knowledge spheres, for example: book clubs, community and campus learning spaces, and any spaces that celebrate intellectual and scholarly activism that can serve as a support, motivation, and empowerment space for you.)

_____

_____

_____

_____

Once you have a deeper understanding of the various avenues in which you can engage in activism, you can intentionally identify what support systems are on campus or in your community, and most importantly, what support needs to be enacted for you to thrive.

CHAPTER EIGHT

Locate the Barriers

In this space you are in, you are actively healing, leaning into your natural wiring, investigating how you should navigate your calling, and building on your community of support. It is necessary to identify the barriers you will ultimately overcome in your fight for social justice.

These barriers can be quite diverse and can include:

- Familial barriers

- Community barriers

- Historical barriers that have oppressed communities and identities you are advocating for

- The campus and community climate toward the population, issue, or topic

Familial Barriers

Taking an activist stance has historically come with resistance in the form of racialized incidents, systemic oppression, or lack of support for the individual activist or activist group. Participants in my studies reflected on resistance and pushback toward their activism from various entities. Where family support for some can be a given, others expressed that relationships with their family and loved ones became strained and served as barriers to the growth and development of their activism. Wanting to honor his family by pursuing a degree, Owen experienced internal conflict as he developed into an activist. His mother was a source of his internal conflict that turned into a strained relationship, illustrating generational differences regarding activism in the Black community:

"My mom was always more of the type to say 'Go to school, get your education, get your school paid for, and just play football. And just do everything the right way and don't get angry,' you know? She's from Mississippi and she moved to Chicago in the great migration, so I understand where she's coming from, and she doesn't want my opportunities to be taken away because I don't want to stand with certain people. So, once I got into college and had my own voice, being able to believe my own thoughts, and everything was important to me, it has brought a strain to our relationship."

Edward also experienced strain in the relationship with his parents as he sharpened his activist lens. This led him to seek support and understanding from others:

"My parents are very old-fashioned, so there are some things I say I believe in, that my brothers say and believe in, that my parents don't believe. That's just how they are. They were born so long ago, and they are content with the world that they want to live in, so that's what they do, never make waves. I'm different; I'm not like them."

Parents and caregivers are usually the first beacons of light to their children, telling them they can be anything they want to be, and to live by that in which they believe. As their sons and daughters cultivate their activist identity, ironically, some parents have told them not to do anything to jeopardize their athletic academic scholarships, or position in their sport, thereby leading to relationship strain and dissonance as a cost of activism.

As supportive as Alexandria's mother was in her upbringing, she reflects on instances her mother would speak of her activism, saying to her, "Don't let these protests mess up your opportunity. Don't do anything to jeopardize your scholarship." These types of mixed messages can lead to difficult relationships with the same people who students thought were their biggest fans. Unfortunately, that support can come with conditions that can lead to isolation from those primary support people in an activist's life, serving as another cost of and barrier to activism.

As I experienced personal injustices in my life surrounded by the social and racial inequity happening in society to Black, Indigenous, and People of Color (BIPOC) and the LGBTQIA communities, I also did not receive wholehearted support from people in my family and close community as I grew in my calling to my activism. I experienced a great deal of opposition in relationships that sometimes led to the dissolving of friendships and relationships. That was heartbreaking.

As emerging activists, we are experiencing so many emotions, and the last thing we want is the crumbling of a conditional support system.

I say "conditional" because the support may have been demonstrated as long as we conducted ourselves in a manner that was acceptable to the status quo of preferences and comfort zones. Once we challenged those, that support may have changed, decreased, or outright stopped.

If this has taken place or is happening currently, reflect on these questions to assist in your navigation of these relationships:

Have you experienced strained relationships, lack of support, or outright opposition to your activist lens from family and close friends? From whom?

_____

_____

_____

_____

How have you responded to such barriers?

_____

_____

_____

_____

Do you have safe spaces in your life to discuss your passion and activism that help you to a deeper understanding of family or close friends who oppose your activism?

_____

_____

_____

_____

What strategies are you utilizing to heal from or cope with the lack of support or the barriers you face to your activism?

_____

_____

_____

_____

What other sources of support have you been seeking if your family isn't a part of that ecosystem?

_____

_____

_____

_____

Recognize and Educate Yourself on the Historical Barriers that Have Oppressed Communities and Identities You Are Advocating For

Not only is recognizing the historical barriers crucial to growing as an activist, but, more important, educating yourself on the historical barriers that have oppressed communities and identities you are advocating is key. Allowing yourself to do so can provide deeper context in the fight toward social justice. I learned early in my calling in activism that without education, activism is null and void. An example of this was a beautiful explosion of passion that began to bloom at the beginning of my Ph.D. program, an ecosystem of knowledge within which I curated my academic tenure around activism, which birthed my dissertation.

I was engaged in deep experiential learning that sharpened my activist lens as I continued to build my knowledge on the staggering historical prevalence of racism and anti-Blackness demonstrated in the policies, procedures, and behaviors embedded in society and the campus climate at institutions of higher education. I believe you can experience this deep experiential learning without being in a Ph.D. program or structured learning environment. The more education you have on an issue, topic, or population of interest to you concerning the oppression, racism, and discrimination against such groups, the more you will build a confidence as an activist that does not solely rely on your passion but on the depth of your knowledge. Taking the time to build upon your capacity to learn and grow on a knowledge level will grow your activist identity exponentially.

Additionally, the more knowledgeable you are, the more equipped you will be when the time comes to articulate your "why" for advocating for the population, issue, or topic. These whys can be articulated in more structured settings, such as school or learning communities, or simply in conversation with those who may be opposed to your activism, or also those who are curious and desire to learn more about your journey. You never know when your platform will present itself to educate someone. When Colin Kaepernick was asked after the game why he knelt for the first time during the 2016 NFL season, it was clear he was educated and did the research on the social and racial injustices he was kneeling for. This served as a poignant and compelling blend of his personal experiences on the issues, but also his understanding of the historical background and context of such issues.

To engage in experiential learning in your activism, I encourage you to reflect on these questions:

What knowledge do you already have about the historical barriers that have oppressed communities and identities you are advocating for?

_____

_____

_____

_____

Where did you obtain this knowledge? Was it through personal experience or through external knowledge acquisition?

_____

_____

_____

_____

What are the gaps of knowledge you currently have about the historical oppression, racism, and discrimination against the populations you are passionate about in your activism?

_____

_____

_____

_____

How will having a deeper understanding and knowledge of this history of oppression, racism, and discrimination strengthen you personally as an activist?

_____

_____

_____

_____

The Campus and Community Climate Toward the Population, Issue, or Topic

A common indicator of how a college operationalizes support and what priorities are truly at the helm is the campus climate. Bauer[121] defines *campus climate* as "the current perceptions, attitudes, and expectations that define the institution and its members." Kuh and Whitt[122] introduce the term *campus culture*, which includes the deeply embedded practices, beliefs, and perceptions that shape the behaviors of how individuals and groups interpret their experiences on and off campus. Both definitions provide a broader picture of the norms the campus is built upon, as campus culture informs campus climate and illustrates a very clear picture of what is valued in institutional integrity.

For the participants in the study, coaches, governing entities, institutions, and community partners did not support their activism, which, in turn, caused turmoil, strife, and isolation. As they were experiencing this, it became blatantly clear that the campus and community climate displayed salient and nonsalient messages supporting this notion of a noninclusive campus climate for those who identify as activists. This is a common barrier and it is imperative to recognize these types of barriers in order to understand how to navigate them and locate opportunities to be an integral part of changing the campus and community climate toward inclusivity and social justice.

When I served as the Director of Student Activities and Community Services at a small faith-based institution, I conducted a campus climate assessment to gauge how welcoming the campus was for Black and African American students and students of color. I did this to be a reformer and to utilize my position to improve the climate, particularly in the Department of Student Affairs. Black and African American students comprised only 6% of the student population, and within that 6%, a majority of the Black and African American students were identified as athletes. Regarding graduation rates, the six-year rate of African American students pursuing a bachelor's degree was the lowest subgroup to graduate—at 33%, which was a cause for alarm.

Although many institutions that offer bachelor's degrees call them a "four-year degree," statistics have shown that the majority of students do not obtain their bachelor's degree in four years, and it is more common to earn it within six years. Because of this, the

United States Department of Education compiles six-year graduation rate data. Similar to national trends, Black and African American students at that university weren't graduating this subgroup of students at a higher rate.

Something taking place within the campus climate was affecting the experiences of Black and African American students.

I conducted focus group meetings for these students to express concerns and share narratives of their experiences at the university. The narratives from the students confirmed that there was an illusion of inclusivity in the campus climate for the Black and African American students, particularly for the athletes the college recruited to play. Because this was a faith-based institution, students were asked to sign a statement of faith but failed to be assisted in the growth of not only their faith identity, but their Black and African American identity (absent mentorship), mainly because of the lack of diversity.

Many of those students expressed that they were ostracized when they had questions regarding certain teachings and experienced the lack of diversity in not only the faith-based courses, but in all curricula. As students inquired and asked about certain cultural programs and support for Black students, administration would reply with "We are all God's children," hence creating the illusion that all students were welcome on their campus simply because they were Christian, even though the Black and African American students did not experience such inclusion.

After creating the assessment report and proposing multiple programs, services, and community partnerships to create a more culturally conscious campus, I also faced institutional barriers in my position as Director from leaders who hid under the cloak of Christianity and white privilege. My time there confirmed the importance of recognizing how the campus climate can foster, or fail to foster, a sense of community for certain students as well as professionals in education. This is particularly important information for those who are activists. If individuals are aware of their campus culture before committing to the university, they are better equipped for the barriers they may experience and better prepared to engage in the effort to dismantle or change those barriers.

As mentioned previously, campus culture is made up of the deeply embedded practices, beliefs, and perceptions that shape the behaviors of how individuals and groups interpret their experiences on and off campus. In many institutions, the campus culture of Dominantly White Institutions (DWI) in particular have hidden messages communicating that certain populations are not welcome on campus. This is blatantly shown through the lack of diversity in faculty and staff, programs, curriculum, and support for BIPOC.

A Campus Culture of Isolation as a Response to Activism

As a student activist's commitment to activism and social justice deepens, isolation from others who do not share the same level of commitment or interest in activism occurs. This isolation can come from anyone with whom the activist is in relationship with, such as non-BIPOC or nonactivist counterparts, coaches, or stakeholders. This occurred once Logan began kneeling during the national anthem. The sense of isolation surfaced specifically on her volleyball team, as she was the only Black woman player. No one from her team joined her in kneeling during the national anthem.

As a result of her activism, Logan's coaches, who were all white, while in a tournament during Memorial Day weekend in Texas, asked her instead of kneeling if she could just not put her hand over her heart during the national anthem. They said it was because they wanted everyone to "get back home safe because it was crazy out there." This was a blatant demonstration of white privilege and an abuse of power. This forced decision cost Logan to feel deep conviction and inner conflict. She wanted to kneel but also felt the potential burden and guilt if her teammates were to get injured in the hostile Southern white environment. This incident caused isolation for Logan from her teammates because they could not identify with the importance of kneeling during the national anthem, especially in Texas.

Logan had well-intentioned white individuals in her life, loosely identifying as allies, but they showed their lack of true support explicitly through their actions by creating conflict and making it difficult for her to truly engage in activism. Without their unfiltered support, the result was her isolation from her non-Black counterparts.

The disconnect and lack of support from coaches was another barrier to activism that the study participants identified. College athletes are unlikely to be engaged outside of athletics unless their coaches are supportive. Thus, participants expressed that coaches are unlikely to be supportive of anything that threatens their own career stability.

Similarly, as stated by participants, (a) coaches have seldom shown support for their activist identity, especially if they see this as a distraction; and (b) if the coach is not Black or chooses not to acknowledge and address the issues occurring outside the walls of the athletics department, then these factors impact a Black college athlete activist's experiences. These practices are a prime example of isolation and lack of support as a practice of an oppressive campus climate led by the decision-makers on campus.

One participant shared his experiences with his coach and the lack of support for his activism and overall disconnect:

> "I think there needs to be more consistent communication between the coaches, coaching staff, and athletes. I think there just needs to be more communication, generally, someone checking in on you and what you're passionate about other than your sport, like activism. I think the coaching staff should be open to spending a little more time doing that. When an athlete has a strong relationship with their coach, on a coaching level and even more on a personal level, they feel supported in all aspects of their life, and, in turn, has a stronger drive to succeed under that coach. That's what is missing, and there lies the disconnect."

Many institutions of higher education and athletic departments, particularly coaches, see athletes for their athletic prowess first and worry secondly about keeping them academically eligible. Fostering other realms of athletes' identities, such as their activist identities, serves no purpose and has no relevance for winning games; therefore, institutions do not benefit from athletes developing an activist identity and engaging in activism.

Keith reflected on how his coaches have attempted to marginalize him to solely identify as an athlete:

> *"Coaches have said that I should just stay in my athlete lane and just focus on my sport, especially during the season. Coaches and different people in the athletics department have been telling me that I shouldn't do what I do [activism], because they think it's been a distraction.... But I will continue to engage in activism anyway."*

The coach is an individual who, to the athlete, is perceived as a supporter. If the coach is white or uninformed of the issues pertaining to the communities from which the athlete hails, this can isolate the athlete activist, resulting in a fragmented relationship between the two and demonstrating isolation as a response to activism, further creating an unwelcome campus climate.

As you recognize the barriers in your quest toward social justice, here are questions to ask yourself and to investigate:

Who and what are the opposers of the causes and identities that are important to you?

_____

_____

_____

_____

What do people who disagree with you not know or understand about your issue?

_____

_____

_____

_____

Who benefits from the status continuing on as it is, and how?

_____

_____

_____

_____

How have you or others attempted to dismantle or chip away at these barriers?

_____

_____

_____

_____

What tactics can you utilize that have worked for individuals and communities gaining victories against these opposers? What didn't work so well that you can learn from?

_____

_____

_____

_____

Ultimately, as you recognize the barriers, where can you see yourself making a difference in breaking and challenging these barriers?

_____

_____

_____

_____

CHAPTER NINE

Practice Radical Self-Compassion and Care

Over the past seven years, college students' commitment to activism in political and civic engagement continues to soar. In recent years, studies by UCLA's Higher Education Research Institute found the highest percentage of the study's history of incoming students proclaiming they'd participate in protests and some form of activism in their collegiate careers.[123] With the surge of activism, taking care of oneself must be radical as you step boldly into your fight for equity and equality.

> *We are in the process of creating a world in which we recognize every individual's right to receive love, care, and respect, and failing to receive that can take a toll on your mind, body, and soul.*

This tenet is called Practice Radical Self-Compassion and Care because taking care of yourself is crucial to being able to resist oppression and injustice. The effects of entities on campus attempting to disrupt activism, especially toward those who attended or worked at Dominantly White Institutions (DWIs), has had many adverse effects on individuals striving for equity and social justice. These effects have ranged from a sense of "onlyness" and "racial battle fatigue" to activist burnout and overall mental health strain.

Harper et al.[124] defined "onlyness" as the psycho-emotional burden of having to strategically navigate a racially politicized space occupied by few peers, role models, and guardians from one's same racial or ethnic group. The student and athlete activists in my studies described experiencing onlyness on their teams, in classroom settings, and in the community, leaving them unsupported and without a critical mass of other activists on campus with whom to congregate and fellowship. The feeling of onlyness and isolation are prime examples of the unique intersection of when race, identities, athletic position, and activist identity are intertwined, especially when the displaying of such identities do not align with the institution's makeup and mission.

As isolation and onlyness were identified as the overarching emotional and psychological effects of activism expressed by participants, previous research and my findings link isolation to a gauntlet of other racialized problems—one in particular referred to as racial battle fatigue (RBF). Smith[125] coined the phenomenon as racial battle fatigue due to the physical and psychological toll endured by people of color because of the constant discrimination, microaggressions, and stereotyping threats they experience. Black, Indigenous, and People of Color (BIPOC) in multiple walks of life experience RBF while navigating white or majority-white spaces, especially as they lean into their activist identity in white spaces.

Kristin expressed experiencing personal tragedies related to gun violence and wished she had support from coaches and her athletic department, but instead had to decide to weather those storms alone. That, in turn, manifested into bouts of anxiety and depression. On February 14, 2018, a gunman opened fire at Marjory Stoneman Douglas High School in Parkland, FL, killing 17 students and staff members and injuring 17 others. As the world watched in agony, Kristin also watched this unfolding with a personal tie to the school, as she is from Miami and still had loved ones who were current students at the school.

Additionally, feelings of isolation can also lead to activist burnout. Converging the experiences of participants to previous research, the activists I worked with experienced isolation that manifested into activist burnout because of the lack of support and community of other activists at their institutions. Similarly, Gorski[126] found in a study of social justice education activists in the United States that burnout among all participants occurred. Gorski's[127] studies revealed similar findings, that activist burnout was rooted in racist backlash from entities attempting to disrupt their activism, especially those who attended or worked at Predominantly White Institutions (PWIs).

In the same way, Pines[128] found once-dedicated activists shared that they began to "lose their spirit" and disengage due to the physical and emotional tolls activism took on them. Similar to the aforementioned research, almost all participants in the study attended a DWI or PWI. In addition to experiencing activist burnout, the student and community activists expressed a deep sense of compassion fatigue,[129] the idea that one can get exhausted from caring so much. Perhaps the most insidious aspect of compassion fatigue is that it attacks the very core of what brings individuals into activist work—their empathy and compassion for others.

Mental Health Issues as a Result of Racism and White Supremacy

A majority of participants expressed experiencing some form of racialized psychological damage, having to navigate the many unwelcoming spaces on campus for many of their identities.

> *People of color, particularly Black people, pay heavy psychological dues in attempting to balance two worlds—the one into which they are born and the one the world presents to them.*

The experience can lead to considerable stress, tension, and frustration. In fact, W. E. B. Dubois[130] explained this manner of adjustment among Black individuals in what he calls double consciousness:

> *"It is a peculiar sensation, this double consciousness, this sense of always looking at one's self through the eyes of others, of measuring one's soul by the tape of a world that looks on with amused contempt and pity. One ever feels twoness—an American, a Negro; two souls, two thoughts, two unreconciled strivings; two warring ideals in one dark body, whose dogged strength alone keeps it from being torn asunder."*

One of only seven Black students at their school as a child, with half of the children being his kin, Edward was no stranger to racism and feelings of isolation that led him and his siblings to fight for a place in society. Being raised in a Pacific Northwest city and of African and German descent, both he and his siblings were singled out in many altercations where race resided at the forefront:

> "In high school, there was lots of racism and discrimination I felt and situations that all three of us (siblings) had to go through. So, when it came down to it, there's one thing about being African and then there's another about being Black.... You don't know where you're from. You don't have that sense of self-pride. You don't have that self-identity. It's been stripped away from you. I have a lot of people tell me I'm wrong. They tell me I'm that angry Black dude. I've had people try to take my voice away from me and tell me that I'm not allowed to speak."

Similar to the blatant racism and microaggressions Edward experienced, Darren reflected on an incident that continued to illuminate anti-Blackness and police brutality for him:

> "I was in the elevator one time and this white lady was in there as well, and she immediately moved to the other side when I got in. She probably thought I was going to do something to her, but in reality, it wasn't about any of that. But that's not true. I'm just here trying to go to where I need to go, that's it. I had another issue when I was at Chipotle, and there was an officer in there ordering food ... and he kept looking at us a certain way with his hand on his hip as if he was about to reach for his gun. So, it was like one of those things where we got to play it cool and just relax, do not do anything out of the ordinary. So, I didn't look at him or anything. I just focused on ordering my food. And you look at other people and it's like they don't have to go through this. The fact that in certain scenarios and situations, their life and safety aren't put in jeopardy, while if you're Black, it is; now that's frustrating."

As these occurrences of injustices take place in society and to them personally, to activists the act of burnout happens frequently. This exhaustion can cause activists to close the doorways to their heart. Therefore, activists can only be their best selves if their emotional, physical, and psychological needs are met with self-care at the root of those fulfilled needs. The very act of self-care is a rejection of cruelty, discrimination, and oppression and is crucial to being able to resist injustice.

Creating a Radical Self-Care and Compassion Plan

Self-care strategies must be at the forefront of the plan for activists' emotional health and wellness, as they navigate campus with multiple identities, but also with an activist identity. These experiences can take a toll in navigating one's everyday life as an activist. In addition, for an activist of color or other minoritized groups, it is crucial for these individuals to get their basic needs met to flourish.

> *Identifying support for activists is imperative, but also the foundation of support must include focusing on mental health, emotional health, and well-being.*

Over the years, some of my study participants shared self-care strategies that worked for them as they navigated their growth in activism, while others struggled to identify ways to cultivate their deep care and compassion. Harkening back to Maslow's Hierarchy of Needs, Maslow stated that people are motivated to achieve certain needs and that some needs take precedence over others. Our most basic need is for physical survival, and this will be the first thing that motivates our behavior. Self-care is at the root of meeting those needs. We must treat ourselves the way we want others to be treated if we are true to our beliefs.

I had the pleasure of presenting at the University of the Western Cape in South Africa on self-care strategies for student activists. One of the questions I would ask them would be, "What are you doing for self-care?" From the narratives of the students I worked with, lived experiences, and my personal reflections, utilizing Maslow's Hierarchy of Needs, here are suggestions I presented in South Africa that I encourage you to build on toward deep and radical self-compassion and care.

Meeting Your Basic Needs Toward Radical Self-Compassion and Care: Strategies to Build On

As multiple pandemics are taking place in society and are pulling at your soul, how is this showing up in your emotions and your drive to lean in and use your voice? How are you taking care of yourself and meeting your needs? Suggestions to build on include:

Physiological Needs:

- Get regular exercise.
- Connect with nature.
- Give yourself adequate sleep.
- Consume nutritious food.
- Drink plenty of water.

Safety Needs:

- Unplug from social media.
- Situational awareness: Protect your mental and physical safety in a world where embodying particular identities is not safe in certain spaces in society.
- Limit social gatherings that raise debates; protect your peace and your body.

Love and Belonging Needs:

- An extension of Finding Your People—have a strong support system.
- Engage in prayer.
- Surround yourself with positivity.
- Recognize the validity of your feelings.

Esteem Needs:

- Be kind to yourself.
- Spend time journaling.
- Make use of therapy and meditation apps.

- Practice mindfulness, compassion, and gratitude practices that are helpful in reducing stress and anxiety.
- Give yourself permission to say no.

Self-Actualization:

- As you are working on meeting your physiological, safety, love and belonging, and esteem needs, investigate your mind and body to gauge how well you are rejuvenated and practicing radical care and compassion.
- What are some personal strategies of various types of radical self-care and compassion that have worked and are working for you in this time of racial and social injustice?

Mental care and compassion:

_____

_____

_____

_____

Spiritual care and compassion:

_____

_____

_____

_____

Emotional care and compassion:

_____

_____

_____

_____

Physical care and compassion:

_____

_____

_____

_____

Social care and compassion:

_____

_____

_____

_____

Sensory rest:

_____

_____

_____

_____

Activists strive to bring awareness to social injustice that emphasizes direct, vigorous action, especially in support of or opposition to one side of a controversial issue. This action is exhausting, and it's crucial and necessary to rejuvenate your mind, body, and soul. We need you.

CHAPTER TEN

Change the World!

"Get in good trouble, necessary trouble,
and help redeem the soul of America."
—John Lewis

As you continue to grow and develop in your advocacy and activism, build upon your resources, find your people, boldly face the barriers while radically loving yourself, you have engaged in the practice of being a holistic advocate and activist. Furthermore, when a collective mass of individuals' consciousness is raised to injustices that take place in their community, they are empowered to leave a legacy and uplift their community to demand equity.

Activism continues to be a forum where people, in the face of disagreement, are still utilizing their voices, speaking truth to power, and speaking truth to the masses.

> *Although the form of student activism has expanded,*
> *the function and purpose has not. This is why*
> *activism still matters today. This is why you matter.*
> *Don't give up. Don't ever give up.*

Now that you have the Activism Growth Model™ in your toolbox, where will you go from here?

What is your most impactful takeaway from the first half of this book?

_____

_____

_____

_____

What is your vision of the activist's or your next steps toward a just and fair society?

_____

_____

_____

_____

What do you see as an immediate change that you could work toward growing your activist and advocate identity?

_____

_____

_____

_____

Based on what you have read so far in this book, what do you know about yourself that you did not know before?

_____

_____

_____

_____

PART TWO

For Allies and Accomplices

◇◇◇◇◇◇◇◇◇◇◇◇◇◇◇◇◇◇◇◇◇◇◇◇

CHAPTER ELEVEN

Know Your Role, White Allies and Accomplices: Undoing the Systems that Have Benefited You

Before I get into a deeper discussion of the specific impact made by coaches, teachers, administrators, and institutions in the lives of Black College Athlete Activists, I want to stop and pause to talk about two roles and terms, *ally* and *accomplice*. In Chapter One, I mentioned who this handbook is for and shared the spectrum of individuals who would benefit from this resource. Not only is this handbook for Black, Indigenous, and People of Color (BIPOC) who desire to lean into their activist identity and are searching for guidance in doing so, but also for their white counterparts who have decided to stand in solidarity with disenfranchised and oppressed groups and use their voices in this fight. Let's talk—this space is for you.

I had the privilege of hearing two of the three co-founders of Black Lives Matter (BLM), Patrisse Cullors and Alicia Garza, speak in 2017 on BLM, social justice, and activism. So many gems were dropped to us, but there was something Cullors said that was so poignant. She spoke on allies versus accomplices, which changed my lens on those terms completely. Mainstream media and the current movement toward social justice needs all entities to engage in dismantling white supremacy and oppressive systems that infiltrate all realms of society. However, there are two very different roles that our white counterparts play, and I would like to unpack these terms before moving further.

There is a stark difference between an ally and an accomplice. An ally has been the most prominent and mainstream term for a white counterpart who self-identifies as someone who is continuing to become educated about racial issues and supporting anti-racism efforts through action by standing with an individual or a group in a marginalized community.

A common example in recent times of allyship has been seen through sports at the collegiate and professional level. For instance, during the national anthem, Black players were kneeling as a white ally is standing next to them with a hand on their shoulder or locking arms with them. Oh, what a photo opportunity, such a powerful image, right? Not quite.

Another example of allyship is white educators or individuals in the community creating book clubs to read the multitude of anti-racism and anti-oppression books to support BIPOC and LGBTQIA authors. In another example, Netflix, the worldwide streaming service, reported an exorbitant increase in viewership by 4,665% in three weeks of the 2016 Ava DuVernay–directed documentary, "13," which perfectly demonstrated the historical intersection of race, justice, and mass incarceration in the U.S.[131] This surge in the rate of viewership of the documentary took place during the summer of 2020 as mass demonstrations took place across the U.S. and the world against systemic racism and police brutality.

Many of my fellow BIPOC colleagues and friends and I received numerous texts, calls, and emails from white friends and colleagues expressing remorse, anger, sadness, shock, and disbelief after not only watching the documentary, but also watching videos of the lynchings of George Floyd and Ahmaud Arbery. Educating yourselves, white friends, is a good start, but this movement calls for more depth of action, like the large numbers of white allies at demonstrations and protests—more than recent times have witnessed.

In an interview in the *San Francisco Chronicle*,[132] East Oakland activist John Jones III had a request for white allies who want to show their support at protests: "Don't hold up a sign that says, 'I can't breathe.' This is not about you. I'm the one who can't breathe."

Being an ally is more than just going to the protests. If you identify as an ally, these are what suggestions of additional actions can look like:

- Listen more than you speak.
- Don't assume you know everything.
- Allow BIPOC to lead.
- Stay in your lane.
- Don't get defensive when you don't know everything.
- Apologize when you get something wrong.
- Remember that being an ally isn't about you or your feelings.
- Don't expect a standing ovation for not being racist.

> *The line between an ally and an accomplice is demonstrated in what one does with the deep discomfort in recognizing systems that you have historically benefited from.*

An ally still has the privilege and choice whether to engage in activism and advocacy, while the accomplice actively dives completely in the trenches with the minoritized and disenfranchised groups. At a speech at Barnard College in 1979, Toni Morrison said, "The function of freedom is freeing someone else." That is what an accomplice does.

An accomplice actively engages in dismantling the structures that oppress the individual or group, where the work is directed and led by the marginalized individual or group. How will you do this as an accomplice? Utilize your privilege, which you have in one way, shape, or form.

I have heard white folks express that they grew up in lower socioeconomic neighborhoods, or were raised by a single parent, and feel they had no privilege. In those moments, I reflect on the quote I once heard: "White privilege doesn't mean your life hasn't been hard. It just means the color of your skin isn't one of the things that makes it harder."

> *White allies, are you down to forgo your privileges, position, status, and the advantages that are not given to minoritized or marginalized groups?*

That's the difference; that's where the line is drawn, operating in the space where you are actively risking it all and pushing past that comfortable feeling of attending a protest, posting a black block on your Instagram, or simply reposting a post from a BIPOC activist. It is more. It is so much more.

I think about the Civil Rights Movement and the diversity of white and BIPOC marching, reforming, agitating, and serving as change agents to dismantle systems of racism, oppression, and white supremacy—a diversity that was an integral factor in the passing of the Civil Rights Act of 1964 and the Voting Rights Act of 1965. It was quite beautiful.

One accomplice who has been highlighted in documentaries and films on the Civil Rights Movement was James Reeb, a white Unitarian Universalist minister, pastor, and activist during the Civil Rights Movement in Washington, D.C., and Boston, MA. He is deemed an accomplice because even before he marched in Selma, AL, for African American voting rights, he gave up his white privilege in many sectors, and lived, with his wife and four children, in lower socioeconomic neighborhoods where many Black and African Americans resided. He did this to connect and understand inequities and oppression. Additionally, he utilized his privilege to encourage his parishioners to be a part of the Civil Rights Movement, jeopardizing his status as a white minister.

Reeb embodied the role of an accomplice on March 9, 1965, because after eating dinner at an integrated restaurant, he was followed and beaten by white men for his support of African American rights. Sadly, he went into a coma and died two days later from his injuries. His death resulted in a national outcry against white supremacy, especially in the Deep South. Reeb put his status, reputation, and consequently his life on the line to fight white supremacy.

A modern-day example of accomplices is a group called White People 4 Black Lives (WP4BL), www.awarela.org, a white anti-racist collective that operates within a national network of white anti-racists called Showing Up for Racial Justice (SURJ) and in alliance with Black Lives Matter: Los Angeles, the Movement for Black Lives (M4BL), and other partners. These are groups of individuals, some in the public eye as actors, directors, and individuals with a great deal of influence in Hollywood as well as accomplices from all walks of life, ready to forgo their status and privilege of being white to stand up against racism and for social justice. Their work includes fundraising, internal and external education, mobilization, recruitment and networking, action planning, and overall taking active risks, particularly in white spaces that must be infiltrated to educate and eradicate oppressive and noninclusive practices.

These accomplices believe strongly that white individuals can play a progressive and supportive role in amplifying the voices and demands of Black people, moving the white community to take a more active and participatory stance for racial justice, and apply strategic pressure on institutions to change racist policies.

If this is an organization that as a white accomplice you may feel called to, I would suggest looking further into getting involved in this organization or ones similar to it in your area. The time is now to be active in your resistance and the decentering of your privilege. We all have a space in this fight for justice.

Not sure where you are in the spectrum of being an ally or an accomplice? Ask yourself these questions, reflect on your answers, and build upon them:

How have you fostered trust through accountability with someone who is Black, Indigenous, or a Person of Color? If so, how can you identify that you have fostered trust?

_____

_____

_____

_____

How have you continually supported Black-owned businesses, authors, or entrepreneurs in the past (3) months?

_____

_____

_____

_____

Identify at least (3) ways in the next month you can actively position your privilege as an opportunity to utilize your voice in predominantly white spaces to eradicate nonequitable areas.

_____

_____

_____

_____

Join or start a group or committee that addresses issues of equity, diversity, and inclusivity in your sphere of influence. Who would you invite?

_____

_____

_____

_____

How many difficult conversations with other white people in your ecosystem have you had to bring about issues of inequity, racism, and oppression? That's a great start—now have more.

CHAPTER TWELVE

Serving Specialized Activist Populations:
Black Athlete Activists and Activists of Color

The first part of this handbook serves as a guidepost for individuals desiring to sharpen their activism by exploring their calling, specific roles, and vehicles to their activism while discovering which barriers to overcome while building their community and self-care plan. The second part of this handbook is curated for those who may or may not identify as activists but desire to engage, learn from, support, and empower Black athlete activists and activists of color.

The motivation behind activism for both professional and amateur athletes is as important as the activism itself—ongoing discrimination that has plagued Black communities and other communities of color for decades. Similar to the impact of the Black Lives Matter movement on the broader U.S. society in the 21st century, Black and African American athletes from the younger generation to the professional ranks utilized their platform as athletes in ways that mirror the Black Campus Movement and athletes of the Civil Rights Movement[133] by utilizing sit-ins, peaceful protests, and nonviolent methods, and, most important, their athlete status to bring about the awareness of the continual injustices plaguing Black communities and communities of color.

Black professional and college athletes were a pivotal piece of the Civil Rights Movement and Black Campus Movement, and they continue to be critical to present-day activism.[134] The 1960s was a decade where there was a shift in Black athletes' consciousness, where they aligned with Civil Rights leaders and other Black student activists. Black athletes were heavily influenced by their nonathlete peers who were engaged in the struggle for human and civil rights by an insurgency in cultural empowerment in a myriad of ways that challenged dominant white norms.[135]

Furthermore, the death of young Black men, women, and boys at the turn of the 21st century has shifted from shocking and predictable. Huey P. Newton in *Revolutionary Suicide* spoke of the unfailing power and influence Black people have once they engage in activism, proclaiming "Black men and women who refuse to live under oppression are dangerous to white society because they become symbols of hope to their brothers and sisters, inspiring them to follow their example" (p. 21). In the same vein, activism over time has changed, and in the 21st century, it has taken on new forms, but the purpose and reason for activism has not.

Relatedly and aforementioned, former NFL quarterback Colin Kaepernick utilized the activism vehicle of kneeling to protest against social injustice, especially the deaths of African Americans at the hands of police as well as the unfair treatment and lack of support of veterans.[136] He and other athletes who utilized kneeling as a form of protesting were referred to as disrespectors of the American flag or sons of bitches by the president of the United States and those who subscribe to that racist and skewed view of patriotism.

Comparatively, one population that has a considerable impact on their campus and community are Black College Athlete Activists (BCAAs) who use their platform for social change. Academic institutions are a crucial component of activism and students have an impact on that culture and climate of their college campuses.[137]

> *Ironically, higher education has attempted to portray that college athletics is a shield from societal and racial injustices by promoting the facade of sports as the great equalizer for all athletes—a grave falsehood.*

As this population of students navigates the campus, their educational experiences are impacted by their race, gender, and status as athletes. Structural influences, such as institutional racism, discrimination, and status, work together to sway the behaviors and experiences of Black college athletes.[138] Conversely, Black college athletes are arguably among the most essential players in this generation's racial justice agenda and fight to recognize and dismantle anti-Blackness,[139] and this has been illustrated in a variety of ways.

As they relate to modern-day college athletes, collective responses to social injustices have been illustrated through kneeling or sitting during the national anthem, wearing paraphernalia on their jerseys and athletic gear with messages such as "Hands up, don't shoot," "I can't breathe," or "Black Lives Matter," bringing attention to the injustices taking place in real time to Black bodies. This has also been illustrated by college athletes utilizing their voices when given opportunities through interviews, team meetings, and other public settings where they are expected to shut up and just play their sport, which is a beautiful act of defiance.

> *Perhaps one of the most visible instances of modern-day Black college athlete activism was the University of Missouri football team.*

In 2015, the University of Missouri's Black football players threatened a boycott of their games in support of the protests regarding racial injustices on their campus. The University of Missouri had been experiencing a slew of racist incidents toward Black students that sparked a hunger strike by a graduate student named Jonathan Butler.[140] Spurred by the mishandling of racial tensions on campus, Butler vowed he would not eat until the university's president, Timothy Wolfe, resigned. On November 8, 2015, Black football players at Mizzou joined the protest and announced they would not practice or play until Wolfe resigned.[141]

This decision would cost the university an exorbitant fine for forfeiting an upcoming game against Brigham Young University later that week. Thirty Black football players linked arms with Jonathan Butler in their demand for Wolfe's resignation, and on November 9, 2015, Wolfe announced his resignation. The 2015 football team offered an outstanding display of the power of Black college athlete activism. The following boycott resulted in a wave of athletes' activism that flooded the nation, illustrating the power of BCAAs.[142]

For some institutions, college athlete activism can be viewed as a misalignment to their so-called mission and vision. Because of this, BCAAs' actions on and off the court or field are roften scrutinized when they do not align with the larger institutional narrative. For instance, in 2017, Louisiana State University's (LSU's) athletic department sent out an email to all its athletes in the wake of Alton Sterling's death at the hands of police the prior year, urging athletes that if they chose to express their opinion on this issue, including on social media, to not wear LSU gear or use LSU branding.[143]

Expanding the realm of Black football and basketball players engaging in activism, Black cheerleaders also engaged in activism by using their visibility and platform. This was demonstrated in the 2017 athletic season when five Black cheerleaders at Kennesaw State, a public university in Georgia, attracted controversy by kneeling during the national anthem to protest police brutality.[144] Following the protests of the cheerleaders, KSU received threats to the university to pull funding from stakeholders, claiming the cheerleaders' actions were unpatriotic. These threats forced the administration to acknowledge the cheerleaders' activism, leading it to change policy, keeping cheerleaders from coming out onto the field until after the national anthem as an attempt to silence their platform and eliminate such perceived disruption.

This unique population of BCAAs has the ability to bring attention to larger societal issues, using their visibility as a platform to create greater awareness of injustice. They have an imperative to speak for those who don't have a voice, and they play a significant role in the struggle for social justice. The intersection of race and athletic position is intertwined in the BCAA's identity. Therefore, capturing the lived experiences and narratives of Black college athletes engaging in activism at such a crucial time in history was at the forefront and impetus of my research and was the motivation to create this model for those who are stakeholders and interact with BCAAs as well as with activists of color.

CHAPTER THIRTEEN

A Multifaceted Support Strategy:
The Black Athlete Activist Leadership Model™ (BA²L)

The college campus environment is a prime location and ripe with opportunity for Black College Athlete Activists (BCAAs) to engage within their campus community and beyond. They can gain a sense of belonging, identity, and development as activists, and hone critical life and civic engagement skills that they may not necessarily obtain within the confines of the classroom. Indeed, collegiate athletes are learning a critical life lesson about using their platforms and celebrity to raise social concerns, rather than merely reap the financial benefits that may come with fame and success.

However, Black athletes are faced with a great deal of racialized challenges as they navigate through a dominant white society. These challenges can include cultural stereotyping, limited positive role models, and violence against their communities—challenges that often lead to difficulties in school. As these themes emerged in my studies, it became apparent that BCAAs were not supported by their institutions in their activist identity as it intersected with their athlete status. This resulted in isolation and a host of difficulties and hardships they experienced as a cost of their activism. Campuses historically perpetuating anti-Blackness prohibited BCAAs from engaging in activism and thriving holistically on their campuses. As a result of this lack of support, cognitive and identity dissonance manifested as participants disclosed a need to be recognized in all their identities as they intersected with their activism.

Therefore, a multifaceted strategy and framework is necessary in order for college athlete activists to receive holistic support as they navigate their prospective campuses and develop their activism. Emerging from my research and analysis of the BCAAs I worked with, the Black Athlete Activist Leadership Model™ (BA²L) was birthed. This model is an invitation for athletic departments, student services, and higher education practitioners, and anyone who serves this population to gain a deeper and informative understanding and support of BCAAs, using a holistic lens and approach.

Based on the narratives and realities of the BCAAs, I posit that utilizing these suggested pillars in the model will allow BCAAs to operate and navigate their campuses, feeling empowered and invigorated by those who serve them:

(a) Viewing athletes as leaders
(b) Embracing intersecting identities
(c) Accounting for campus climate
(d) Incorporating holistic support

No model currently exists to support and develop the leadership of BCAAs holistically from the individual, programmatic, and systemic levels. Ultimately, the BA²L model enables a framework and suggested outline for curricular and co-curricular programming, support, and resources for BCAAs' institutions, truly embodying a holistic approach to their growth and leadership development as activists.

The more informed that institutional stakeholders are about the lived experiences of BCAAs in times of racial and social injustice, the more this knowledge will enable them to systematically create safe spaces for this population. By utilizing the BA²L model, those who serve this population can use their privilege and resources to create welcoming environments for BCAAs to exercise their freedom of speech and continue to develop in their activism (see the figure on the next page).

Viewing Athletes as Leaders

College athletics are a natural breeding ground for leadership, as athletes are constantly navigating challenging situations on the court and the field through victory and defeat. In fact, Nelson[145] posited that student leaders should possess these six leadership skills:

(a) Communication
(b) Decision-making
(c) Organizing
(d) Action planning
(e) Strategic thinking
(f) Risk management

Black Athlete Activist Leadership Model™

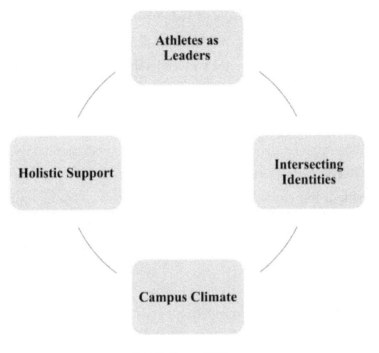

© 2019, George-Williams

Subsequently, college athletes must demonstrate these skills daily in practice and in competition to complete the shared mission of their sport with their teammates. Naturally, because of their leadership abilities, college athletes who identify as activists would also be profound leaders. Although some of the most well-equipped leaders in higher education are athletes, they are not perceived this way and are discounted outside of their locker rooms.

Participants in my studies were engaged in grassroots activism, spearheading and creating organizations and associations geared toward cultivating the needs and centering the experiences of Black college athletes on their respective campuses. Because of their leadership skills, these students obtained advisors and funding, and with each meeting, attendance and visibility increased for the student group. This illustrated a prime example of the aforementioned leadership skills Nelson suggested student leaders should possess.

Another example that emerged from my research that supported that athlete activists are student leaders were the various campus leadership roles some participants held in student government, organizations, and associations that aligned with various identities with which they identified or advocated. These students were aware of their positionality and utilized such influence and leadership to impact change on their campuses—the epitome of a student leader.

Institutions have constructed their own definition of inclusivity and who student leaders are, demonstrated by the lack of support for BCAAs that bled into the campus culture. Recontextualizing student leadership to embrace athlete activism as a form of leadership is imperative to truly embody inclusivity as a practice in higher education. Higher education institutions must examine their current policies and procedures that support or hinder student activist efforts that exclude them from being recognized as student leaders.

It is critical that higher education administrators reframe their gaze on Black athletes and recognize that they are undoubtedly student leaders who deserve adequate support and development. This shift in perspective is the impetus of recontextualizing student leadership in higher education and is the first pillar in this leadership model. Furthermore, this leadership model can be utilized in student leader support, training, and leadership development for BCAAs on the individual, team, programmatic, departmental, or institutional level. By and large, this recognition of BCAAs as student leaders must incorporate an understanding of the underpinning of intersecting identities BCAAs embody once they arrive on campus, which will be examined next in the second pillar of this leadership model.

CHAPTER FOURTEEN

Embracing Intersecting Identities

The guiding conceptual framework for the Black Athlete Activist Leadership Model™ (BA²L) as well as the Activism Growth Model™ (AGM) is critical race theory (CRT).[146] As aforementioned, CRT studies the intersection of race, racism, and power and strives to uncover how oppression of people of color has been established and perpetuated.

The major strength of CRT is the focus on intersectionality with other oppressed identities, such as gender, sexual orientation, or class, as it factors in the experiences of Black, Indigenous, and People of Color (BIPOC). The purpose of using this framework was to give voice to BIPOC in my studies by documenting and understanding their stories and journeys toward social justice advocacy through their activism.

Not only is recognizing, honoring, and centering all of the salient and nonsalient identities of Black College Athlete Activists (BCAAs) critical for comprehensive understanding of such populations, this honoring of their identities will strengthen and empower BCAAs' commitment to social justice, and one of the foundational bookends of my research and this text.

When examining the lived experience of Black Female College Athlete Activists (BFCAAs), Black Feminist Thought (BFT) was considered a conceptual framework for the BA²L model and the AGM, as the framework was utilized in my research's analysis of the female participant narratives that motivated the creation of my activism models.

Black Feminist Thought is committed to social justice, emancipation, and the empowerment of oppressed women of color.[147] Correspondingly, BFT focuses Black and African American girls' and women's experiences[148] and empowers them with the right to interpret their reality and define their experiences, and "links Black and African American women's oppression to activism."[149]

By utilizing BFT as a conceptual research framework, scholars, especially Black women activists and scholars, can rearticulate a Black woman's standpoint by being rooted in the everyday experiences of those women.[150] The major characteristics of BFT are (a) the lived experience as a criterion of meaning and (b) using dialogue in assessing knowledge claims,[151] which align with the goals of my research, the building of the activism models, and are also known as experiential knowledge or counternarratives in CRT. Similarly, focusing on Black women's narratives supports Crenshaw's[152] sentiment of intersectionality and empowerment.

Crenshaw echoed those sentiments as she shared at the fourth annual Her Dream Deferred Conference on the status of Black women and girls in April 2018 in Washington, D.C., in partnership with the African American Policy Forum (AAPF): "We must begin to tell Black women's stories because, without them, we cannot tell the story of Black men, white men, white women, or anyone else in this country. The story of Black women is critical because those who don't know their history are doomed to repeat it."

Therefore, making space to understand intersectionality through the lens of BFT provides a powerful framework for inserting the voices, cultures, and experiences of Black women into the academy and other institutions of knowledge production.[153]

> *When I had the pleasure of spending time with Black female activists, it continued to support the notion that this group of activists has had a long history of resistance and struggle, and still remain an unsung group.*

Therefore, their distinctive narratives and experiences deserve to be heard and honored by understanding their stories and journeys toward social justice advocacy through their activism.

Likewise, Bailey, a senior student activist, recognized the necessity to acknowledge and center Black women's voices as she experienced this in the classroom and on campus as a Black woman:

> "I feel like disagreeing with a man, let alone a white man, is such a large thing that doesn't take place often. Sometimes in class, I feel like I'm talking too much sometimes, so, I'm like, I'm going to talk a little less. But I realize that being a Black woman, you have to be the first step in a lot of places. One way is using your voice in any environment that you don't commonly see yourself in. Just being a Black woman, being an athlete, also being an intellectual, just being here on campus, you're marginalized in a lot of different spaces. And as Black women, our voices are not necessarily heard all the time here, and when it is, it is in such a way where a lot of people would discount it. And I think that, my worldview, my womanhood, and my Blackness have really played a role in how other people have viewed me, and how I view the world."

Kristin, a sophomore soccer player, speaks to the experiences with her white male coach, where he was clueless that his actions were racist and sexist:

> "I almost got in a fight because of a racial and sexist slur someone called me, and my coach did nothing. I don't know if that response was because he's not from a minority group and he's not a female. So, he wouldn't understand where I was coming from to begin with. Honestly, it makes me more empowered because I am facing two oppressions, coming from two underrepresented groups. So, I feel like there is a need for me to be more active in my community to paint a positive representation of my two groups I identify with. Some people that I meet, I change their mind about gender or racial stereotypes and I affect their opinion. So, I feel a sense of responsibility to care for myself, not just as an athlete but as a Black woman."

Historically, Black and African American athletes' experiences have been intersected by race and gender ideology within the dominant culture,[154] which in many spaces are predominantly white.

> *Therefore, creating spaces for Black College Athlete Activists to authentically share their entire selves and not hide or diminish parts of their identity takes effort from those who embody majority identities.*

This does not have to solely mean white majority, but heterosexual, cisgender individuals, especially those in leadership roles at institutions and athletic departments who must communicate and learn about the experiences of the athletes of color and other marginalized identities and groups on campus. This is especially imperative when examining the campus climate BCAAs experience throughout their collegiate career.

In summary, an incorporation of this leadership model that explicates the cruciality of acknowledging all the identities BCAAs bring onto their campuses creates a space for higher education practitioners to embrace an opportunity for a more comprehensive understanding of these student leaders. Moreover, as a deeper understanding of their intersecting identities occurs, curricula can be birthed to honor the activist histories from which their identities hail, as well as provide opportunities for dialogue and programming on the individual, team, program, departmental, and institutional levels. Once there is a comprehensive understanding of the intersecting identities BCAAs embody, an interrogation of the climate in which they are navigating on such campuses in those identities should be explored as the third pillar in this leadership model.

CHAPTER FIFTEEN

Account for Campus Climate

Cooper et al.[155] asserted, when examining African American athlete activists' actions by, for, and through athletics/sport, that it is important to understand the connection between inequities in both society and sport. This type of inequality and unwelcoming campus environment lends to marginalization, fostering a host of emotionally and psychologically distressful outcomes for students of color, especially Black College Athlete Activists (BCAAs).

> *To fully comprehend the lived experiences of BCAAs, one must also gain awareness and understanding of the campus climate in which these students are immersed.*

Cooper's assertion can be supported by examining the campus climate and racial culture of Black athletes' institutions and athletic departments. Comparatively, Quaye, Griffin, and Museus[156] defined campus racial climate as "the current attitudes, perceptions, and expectations within the institutional community about issues of race, ethnicity, and diversity." As it pertains to my studies, athletic activism is also an issue explored as part of the institution's campus racial climate relating to the level of acceptance and support for BCAAs.

These policies can create either a welcoming or unwelcoming environment for students of color; namely, Black college athletes who identify as activists.

Correspondingly, Museus, Ravello, and Vega[157] found campus racial culture is birthed from the campus racial climate that demonstrates collective patterns of beliefs, values, assumptions, and norms that ultimately manifest into the institution's mission, traditions, interactions, language, and artifacts, therefore shaping a student's ability to feel welcome on campus.

Once Edward arrived on his college campus, he was faced with blatant microaggressions, this time from a coach in his athletic department. Edward reflected on an incident where his coach used him as a recruiting tool, illustrating a failed attempt at interest convergence and a successful attempt at microaggressing him:

> *"We had a young African American man come to our campus and he [coach] said to the recruit some really ignorant statement like, 'We have another African kid on our team; you should talk to him because he can understand you. He's Black like you.'"*

Although the BCAAs hail from various institutions, participants in my studies revealed commonalities of experiencing campus climates of marginalization and disconnection from the larger student community, especially the Black student activist community with whom they congregate and fellowship.

This is supported by participants sharing examples of norms that had manifested into their athletic departments' and institutions' rules and an inability to support their activism efforts as it conflicted with their athlete status.

> *Participants all reported their activism was not supported and, at some institutions, was prohibited due to contracts, policies, and restraints made so that athletes would conduct themselves in a manner that was supposedly representing the school.*

Interrogating Historically Activist Institutions' Campus Climates for BCAAs

The institutions the majority of participants in my research attended have campus climates that create a culture unwelcoming to their race, gender, and activist identities regardless of various institutional types. These institutional types varied from Predominantly White Institutions (PWIs), Dominantly White Institutions (DWIs), Hispanically Serving Institutions (HSIs), Minority Serving Institutions (MSIs), Historically Black Colleges and Universities (HBCUs), and Historically Activist Institutions (HAIs).

HAI, a term birthed from my data analysis in my research, is a campus with historical roots in student activism in which the traditions, curriculum, pedagogy, and artifacts on campus have illustrated and continue to illustrate campus activism. At HAI campuses, there is an awareness of the institution's history of activism and a pride in representing the institution through its sport as well as the perceived environment that welcomes activism due to its institution's status as an HAI.

Being bound contractually to the university and its proposed values, study participants, especially at HAIs, expressed the lack of support utilizing their voice and engaging in activism, ironically, at an institution rooted in activism but having many restrictions on certain students. Consequently, at an institution with historical roots of student activism and advocacy (i.e., an HAI), many of the BCAAs in my studies were discouraged from engaging in activism. This created a breakdown in communication, understanding, and support from stakeholders.

> *It is because of this truth that the need to be understood, supported, and free to express all their identities is crucial to the overall development and success of BCAAs on campus.*

If this support does not occur, then the repercussions are detrimental to the mind, body, and spirit—essentially, the overall wellness of this group of students.

Incorporating holistic support as part of leadership development and support of BCAAs is imperative for higher education practitioners to understand and support the unique needs of this student group and is discussed in the fourth and final section of this BCAA leadership model.

CHAPTER SIXTEEN

Incorporating Holistic Support for Black College Athlete Activists

Although there is research on ways to support student activists on campus,[158] as previously stated, no framework has yet been created that aids in the holistic development of Black College Athlete Activists (BCAAs) at foundational levels (individual, departmental, and institutional). Therefore, there is a need for a comprehensive array of services and support to address the uniqueness of this student population.

> *As student activism is reemerging in the 21st century, it is increasingly important for higher education practitioners to understand the needs of student activists, particularly BCAAs, and provide the necessary support.*

Once higher education practitioners understand the unique needs BCAAs have to be supported, coalition and collaboration building between multiple entities on campus are imperative. Moreover, this understanding of their needs must be clear enough so that, wherever the BCAA is on campus, their support is demonstrated through partnerships between athletics, academic affairs, and student affairs. The more practical interventions stakeholders and practitioners can implement for a growing population of Black athlete activists, the more progress toward engaging in meaningful and safe experiences for this population can occur.

Another realm of holistic support that should be considered is the emotional health and wellness of BCAAs. BCAAs are perceived as having binary identities, informing expectations that place these students in a box, leaving them fragmented and experiencing dissonance that compromises their mental and emotional health and well-being. Consequently, support groups of this nature are a rare space for college athletes, and particularly athletes of color, to create a space together to discuss the issues of the larger campus culture that, depending on the campus climate of the institution, has historically been stifled from being discussed in the open.

An example of partnerships fostered toward the well-being of BCAAs would be collaboration between the counseling centers on campus. This collaboration would foster a level of normalcy for BCAAs seeking mental health services, as they are plagued with a complexity of experiences due to their various identities. These relationships can be fostered by team and department visits from members of the counseling center, educating them on the array of services offered for their well-being and mental health. Additionally, building partnerships in the community aimed at the well-being of BCAAs could include collaboration with sports psychologists competent in socio-cultural strategies of counseling and psychotherapy. These strategies truly embody providing a comprehensive array of services toward supporting their holistic mental health and wellness.

CHAPTER SEVENTEEN

The BA²L Model in Action: Practical Strategies

As stated in the findings of years of research, the fragmentation of the identities of Black College Athlete Activists (BCAAs) can cause negative experiences throughout their collegiate career. It is crucial for activists to get holistic and comprehensive support in order to flourish on campus. Because of the need for holistic support for this student group, developing comprehensive support of a team of stakeholders and departments on campus is necessary. Among the group of stakeholders that should be highlighted are faculty, coaches, and athletic departments, as they are entities that engage with athlete activists on a frequent basis. Because of the frequent interactions with BCAAs, a heightened accountability is essential, calling for deeper examination and implications for practice. Here are a few suggestions of the BA²L model in action based on consultations I have held with various stakeholders to engage with, educate themselves about, and empower BCAAs.

Heighten Accountability for Faculty, Coaches, and Athletic Departments

In addition to family and community, a college campus consists of a support team of stakeholders. Stakeholders who have frequent contact with this student subgroup can be predictors for success for BCAAs. Because of their proximity to this student subgroup, there is a heightened accountability for specific stakeholders in the support of BCAAs. These are faculty, coaches, and athletic department liaisons. These stakeholders are called to be architects to create diverse opportunities that cultivate spaces of resilience and resistance. They are also called to foster spaces for these students to develop their identities and positionalities.

Educate Faculty on the Reality of Athlete Activists on Campus

Black college athletes, especially those attending Dominantly White Institutions (DWIs), may experience a sense of isolation at a greater level than those who attend universities with a more diverse student body. As participants shared in my research, experiencing isolation, marginalization, and racialized incidents were common because an unwelcoming campus climate increased the likelihood of such occurrences.

Faculty are an underestimated group of stakeholders who can influence the positive climate athlete activists have while navigating campus. Faculty can positively affect the lives of their students by being individuals who can provide direction and guidance outside the realm of athletics.

> *Faculty members must create a safe and welcoming environment for all their students, particularly the largely misunderstood BCAAs, who must navigate assumed biases of their subgroup.*

Consequently, faculty who are not familiar with the background and experiences of this student group should create opportunities to listen to their shared experiences so they can empathize and understand what they endure, especially on campus. Engaging with BCAAs can be done by faculty genuinely asking about particular causes and issues the BCAAs are passionate about so that understanding and possible common ground can be fostered. Interacting and showing interest in BCAAs inside and outside of the classroom demonstrates respect and support for all their identities, whether faculty identify with their activism or not.

Faculty who embody an activist identity are held at a higher level of accountability in their role in fostering a more inclusive campus climate for BCAAs on their campus. These faculty are held at a higher standard particularly because they already embody a level of consciousness of the experiences of BCAAs and other disenfranchised groups and claim to support student activism and advocacy. These faculty members can demonstrate support by continuously engaging with BCAAs through mentorship, attending events held by student organizations that BCAAs belong to or have spearheaded, or even serving as advisors to such organizations.

The more connected the activist faculty are with a heightened sense of consciousness to BCAAs, the more they can provide opportunities and spaces for BCAAs to engage with faculty who do not have the same education, awareness, and relationships with other BCAAs on campus. The activist faculty can serve as gatekeepers to foster a deeper and more comprehensive understanding of the realities BCAAs face on their campus. Consequently, the more faculty are educated regarding this student group, the likelihood of negative interactions and misunderstandings resulting in a negative campus climate can decrease.

Similarly, another important group of stakeholders who have frequent contact with this student subgroup are coaches, who are arguably crucial to the holistic support and reconceptualization of BCAAs.

Engage Coaches to Reconceptualize Athlete Activist Leadership

The influence from the college athletes' coach can have a powerful impact on the college athletes' decisions on an everyday level, affecting their future endeavors. In fact, the coach/player dynamic is arguably one of the most crucial relationships to be fostered while an athlete is in college. The coach is entrusted by the athlete's family to provide guidance, direction, and, in many instances, discipline as a surrogate parent on campus. Due to the large number of single-parent families in the Black community, coaches must recognize that they may be perceived as a parental figure and should operate in the best interests of their athletes.

Coaches must not only stay abreast of the perils of society that may affect the demographics of some of the athletes under their care, but also actively engage in relationship building with the athlete's intersecting identities. This support from a coach can profoundly impact and influence how BCAAs experience their collegiate lives as well as their choice to identify and develop as activists on campus. As coaches are called to support their athletes, especially in all the identities they embody, it is imperative for them to engage in self-reflection of the authenticity of such support.

Suggested topics coaches are encouraged to reflect on are:

What type of flexibility do you have in terms of allowing your athletes to be able to express themselves?

_____

_____

_____

_____

Are you allowing opportunities and spaces to engage in conversations with Black athletes regarding societal issues?

_____

_____

_____

_____

What personal biases, privileges, and blind spots in your identities do you embody that hinder you from being socially conscious?

_____

_____

_____

_____

Utilizing the suggested reflective questions forces coaches to authenticate their intentions but must not stop at the reflective stage. They must be actualized and demonstrated consistently. For example, public displays of activism occur before, during, or after their game or competition, where the coach or coaches are in direct contact with the athlete, allowing immediate opportunities to react to the athletes. In the same way, participants expressed when they've actualized their activism with public displays, their coach or coaches reacted by ostracizing them, penalizing them, or engaging in silence when they were demonized for their activism, which illustrates approval for such demonizing.

Education and training for coaches for a comprehensive understanding of the multiple avenues of athlete activism and, more important, strategies in demonstrating support for public displays of activism by Black athletes are imperative. In these trainings, it is essential to create space for the coaching staff to hear personal narratives of BCAAs who engage in public displays of activism and to express how their coaches can support them.

Coaches have the opportunity to play a crucial role in the support, growth, and development of BCAAs. Yet, the participant narratives illustrated that many coaches shy away from engaging, fostering opportunities to understand, and supporting the efforts of the Black activists on their roster. Although the reasons for the lack of engagement and support vary, the BCAAs in the study shared their perception that disengagement may originate from coaches simply not knowing how to even begin the process of enlightenment and support, especially if they are white or do not identify with BCAAs.

In the sports realm, playbooks, scouting reports, and statistical breakdowns and summaries are embedded in the culture of athletics. Therefore, birthed from the narratives of the desires and wants of BCAAs and utilizing the BA²L model as a guide, an implication for practices leading to the heightened accountability for coaches is the creation of a social justice and activism playbook for coaches.

This playbook can be applied when taking the steps to engage, understand, and explore the various avenues of support coaches can provide that are of value for the BCAAs on their team. Although the coach is a crucial component and figure impacting the experiences of BCAAs, the athletic department is the larger system that must be reconceptualized and held at a higher level of accountability.

Reconceptualize the Role of Athletic Departments

Many study participants expressed that the rules and policies of their athletic departments prohibit them from expressing their activism without being penalized. These barriers cost them opportunities to utilize their positionality to create awareness and make change. Participants expressed experiencing a lack of support to engage in activism from their athletic department, as it may not align with the institution's mission and identity. Nonetheless, the community and nation around the participants was in turmoil and disarray, as racial and social injustices were occurring daily on their campuses and in their communities. Furthermore, policies, procedures, and rules cloaked in anti-Blackness are prohibiting BCAAs from engaging in activism and thriving holistically on their campuses.

Once an examination of stakeholders like faculty, coaches, and athletic departments occurs, it is imperative for specific programmatic ventures to be considered as a call to action for athletic departments to take the lead in implementation. Furthermore, based on the data analysis, recommendations for programming and interventions led by athletic departments are as follows:

- Provide summer or pre-season retreats with entire athletic departments (coaches, staff, and administration) to learn about issues regarding intersecting identities and activism.

- Create collaborations between student affairs and athletic departments to engage in training, workshops, and town halls on issues regarding intersecting identities of Black athletes and activism.

- Form connections between the athletic department and counseling and psychology departments to discuss self-care practices of Black athlete activists to foster holistic support.

- Engage in continuous critical examination of anti-Black and anti-activist policies in the athletic department that hinder and prohibit the expression of Black athlete activists and that conflict with their constitutional freedom of speech.

- Host department-wide microaggression, microinsult, and microinvalidation education and training for coaches and all athletic department staff to create awareness of problematic and microaggressive speech and behavior that marginalize the identities of Black athlete activists on their campuses.

Additionally, based on the data analysis and introduced leadership model, collaborative efforts between the institution's administration and the athletic department are needed for BCAAs to feel supported and recognized as student leaders throughout the campus.

Implications for Interdepartmental Collaborations

As previously mentioned, one of the pillars of the Black Athlete Activist Leadership Model™ (BA²L) focuses on holistic support in which collaborative effort between multiple departments is necessary. The goal of this model is to ensure that regardless of where the athlete activists are on campus, they are supported individually, academically, and from a programmatic standpoint. Therefore, interdepartmental programmatic collaborations and suggested interventions to provide comprehensive support for BCAAs as well as activists of color should be discussed.

Create Brave Spaces for Students to Engage in Activism

As previously identified through participants' narratives, the burden of BCAAs navigating campus with multiple identities creates feelings of marginalization, isolation, and strained relationships, to name a few. Depending on the sport and institution, BCAAs greatly identify with this isolation on their respective teams and in their classrooms. In response to the challenge of isolation and marginalization many Black college athletes experience, these students seek opportunities to engage in activities outside their teams and classrooms. As the emergence of BCAAs continues, student affairs departments, especially housing and residential education, must continue to meet the needs of all students to ensure holistic development as they reside and engage on campus. A recommendation is creating a living community specifically for BCAAs.

On many campuses where a large population of Black athletes attend, there is themed housing for Black students overall, neglecting intersecting identities that reside within a Black student. One of these ignored identities in themed housing for Black students is the Black activist, particularly Black athlete activists. On many residential campuses, athletes are required to live on campus. One suggestion is a living community for BCAAs that provides a space where they can engage and connect with one another from various sports and backgrounds in activism.

A living community specifically for BCAAs would be beneficial for colleges that identify as Historically Active Institutions (HAI). As previously mentioned, HAIs are campuses that have historical roots and engage in student activism and social justice in which the traditions, curriculum, pedagogy, and artifacts on campus illustrate campus activism. The organizations and support should mirror the mission of an authentic HAI by providing a living community for BCAAs, aligning with that institution's mission.

As it pertains to residential experiences, when residential staff are knowledgeable about the sociocultural factors impacting students, and, specifically, Black athlete activists, resources and support are specialized, and students' self-worth, motivation, and overall achievement are enhanced. When residential staff are knowledgeable about the experiences of diverse student populations such as BCAAs, this knowledge can lessen the likelihood of cultural misunderstanding and marginalization. Providing a living space for Black athlete activists embodies that notion.

> *Ultimately, the more practical interventions higher educational practitioners can implement for a growing population of Black athlete activists, the more progress toward engaging in meaningful and safe experiences for this population can occur.*

CLOSING THOUGHTS

Throughout the years, the words from womanist, poet, and civil rights activist Audre Geraldine Lorde have resonated with me:

> *"When I dare to be powerful, to use my strength in the service of my vision, it becomes less and less important whether I am afraid. I began to ask (myself) each time: What's the worst that could happen to me if I tell this truth? Our speaking out will irritate some people, get us called bitchy or hypersensitive and disrupt some dinner parties. And then our speaking out will permit others to speak, until laws are changed, and lives are saved, and the world is altered forever. Next time, ask: What's the worst that will happen? Once you start to speak, people will yell at you. They will interrupt you, put you down and suggest it's personal. And you will lose some friends and lovers and realize you don't miss them. And the world won't end. And new ones will find you and cherish you. And at last you'll know with surpassing certainty that the only one thing more frightening than speaking your truth, is not speaking."*[159]

Lorde's words lit my path and since I began this journey, much has changed within myself, in my family, and in the world. And because of that, I have continued to march, protest, and make space to engage in a multitude of forms of activism and advocacy. Throughout this voyage, I reflected on Lorde's words and pressed on to honor the men and women who have allowed me in their world, if just for a moment.

By recognizing and strengthening my positionality, birthed from my activist DNA, background, experiences as an athlete, and a scholar activist, I have the tools to speak out through my research against anti-Blackness. Like the incredible souls in my studies, I am committed to social justice and utilizing my positionality to challenge systems of oppression and white supremacy. Therefore, this work is not just a researcher gazing upon the other; I am invested in furthering the understanding and awareness of the experiences of Black College Athlete Activists and activists of color. My hope is that this labor of love has served as an ignition, an affirmation, a guidepost, and a handbook in your journey of activism, advocacy, and self-discovery. This is only the beginning.

◇◇◇◇◇◇◇◇◇◇◇◇◇◇◇◇◇◇◇◇◇◇◇◇◇◇◇◇

DEFINITIONS OF TERMS AND ACRONYMS

Activism   Resistance to dominant and/or oppressive culture displayed in a multitude of forms

Activist   An individual who actively campaigns to create political or social change displayed in a multitude of forms

AGM (Activism Growth Model™)   A research-based framework serving as guidance for all who desire to develop, grow, and lean into their activism and advocacy in order to make a difference in their personal lives as well as in the spheres of influence around them and beyond

BA²L (Black Athlete Activist Leadership Model™)   A guide created for those who work with BCAAs, Black student activists, and activists of color as a framework to engage, understand, educate, and support the growth of these groups

BCAAs (Black College Athlete Activists)   Black college athletes who bring attention to larger societal issues, using their visibility as a platform to create greater awareness of injustice

BCM (Black Campus Movement)   A pivotal example of grassroots activism in which the creation of conferences and coalitions formed by Black student activists took place that intertwined with the Civil Rights Movement

BLM (Black Lives Matter)   An international activist movement, rooted in the liberation of Black and African Americans, that campaigns against violence and systemic racism toward Black and African Americans

BPP (Black Panther Party for Self-Defense)   A Black Power political organization founded by college students Bobby Seale and Huey P. Newton in October 1966 in Oakland, CA, centered on Black protection against police brutality, and on Black liberation and advancement

BRS (Black Residential Scholars)   A Living Learning Community to support all Black/African American students and introduce them to campus resources in order for them to successfully navigate the educational experience on campus

BSU (Black Student Union)   An organization dedicated to unifying, uplifting, and empowering Black and African American students on and off campus

College Athletes   College students who participate in an organized competitive sport for the college or university in which they are enrolled

DWI (Dominantly White Institution)   An institution of higher learning that contains a clear majority of spaces, habits, pedagogy, and proportions of faculty, executives, and students who are white

HAI (Historically Active Institution)   A campus with historical roots in student activism in which the traditions, curriculum, pedagogy, and artifacts on campus have illustrated and continue to illustrate campus activism

PWI (Predominantly White Institution)   An institution of higher learning in which whites account for 50% or greater of the student enrollment

Racial Injustice   Inequality or disparity in opportunity, resources, and treatment that occurs as a result of someone's race or ethnicity

RBF (Racial Battle Fatigue)   A term coined to describe the physical and psychological toll endured by people of color because of the constant discrimination, microaggressions, and stereotyping threats they experience

ENDNOTES

1. BLM, 2018
2. Lorde, 1979
3. Dancy, Edwards, & Davis, 2018; Dumas, 2010, 2015, 2016
4. Mills, 1997
5. Coates, 2015; Collins & Jun, 2017; Tait & Van Gorder, 2002
6. Ash, 2018; Dancy et al., 2018; Dumas, 2010, 2015, 2016
7. Solorzano, Allen, & Carroll, 2002
8. Taylor & Clark, 2009
9. Harper, 2012a, p. 10
10. Coates, 2015; Delgado & Stefancic, 2012; Ladson-Billings & Tate, 1995; Lynn & Dixson, 2013; West, 2017
11. Cromer & Millan, 2020
12. Aspen Initiative, 2020
13. Racial Equity Tools, 2020
14. Chambers & Phelps, 1993; Coates, 2015; Rhoads, 1998; Rogers, 2012; Tatum, 1997; West, 2017
15. Biddix, 2014; Biondi, 2012; Cooper et al., 2017; Joyce, 2014; Rhoads, 1998; Rogers, 2012; Shaw, 1996; Washington, 2017; Wiggins, 1992, 2000, 2014
16. Washington, 2014
17. Sampson & Korn, 1970
18. Bradley, 2016; George-Williams, 2019; Rogers, 2012
19. Rye, 2017
20. Rogers, 2012, p. 82
21. George-Williams, 2019; Hulme, 2018
22. MIR, 2017
23. Eagan et al., 2015
24. New, 2016
25. Eagan et al., 2020
26. Babb, 2017; Branch, 2017; Brewer, 2017; Eagan et al., 2015
27. BLM, 2018; Cooper et al., 2017; Edwards, 2016; Rogers, 2012
28. Babb, 2017; Biondi, 2012; Brewer, 2017; Cooper et al., 2017; Lee, 2015; Rhoads, 1998; Rogers, 2012; Washington, 2017
29. Coates, 2015; Rhoads, 1998; Rogers, 2012; Sampson, 1970, Tatum, 1997; West, 2017
30. Walsh, 1981; Washington, 2017
31. Rogers, 2012
32. Duncan, 2018; Edwards, 1969, 1973, 1980; Rogers, 2012
33. Duncan, 2018
34. Rogers, 2012
35. Anderson, 2015; Rhoads, 1998
36. Anderson, 2015; George-Williams, 2019; Rhoads, 1998; Rogers, 2012; Washington, 2014
37. Coates, 2015; Nathan, 2015; New, 2016; Terlep & Belkin, 2015; Tracy & Southall, 2015; West, 2017
38. BLM, 2018
39. Lynn & Dixson, 2013
40. Feagin, 2001
41. Patton, McEwen, Rendón, & Howard-Hamilton, 2007
42. Crenshaw, 1995; Harper & Hurtado, 2011; Ladson-Billings, 1999, 2013; Ladson-Billings & Tate, 1995
43. Ellis, 2004
44. Ladson-Billings, 1995
45. Lynn & Dixson, 2013
46. Yosso, 2005
47. Collins, 2000
48. Collins, 1990b
49. Lindsay-Dennis, 2015; Taylor, 1998
50. Collins, 2000
51. Maslow, 1943
52. Padesky, 2012
53. Centers for Disease Control, 2020
54. Loewy, 2014; Zirwin, 2014
55. hooks, 2013, p. 37

56. Bahadur, 2020
57. Moeschberger et al., 2006
58. Coates, 2015; Rhoads, 1998; Rogers, 2012; Sampson, 1970; Tatum, 1997; West, 2017
59. Cooper et al., 2017
60. Cooper et al., 2017
61. Rhoads, 1998, 2016; Rogers, 2012
62. Anderson, 2015; Rogers, 2012
63. Anderson, 2015, p. 63
64. Anderson, 2015; Flowers, 1998; Rhoads, 1998, 2016; Rogers, 2012
65. Biondi, 2012; Rogers, 2012
66. Biondi, 2012; Rhoads, 1998, 2012; Rogers, 2012
67. Biondi, 2012; Rogers, 2012
68. Biondi, 2012
69. Biondi, 2012; Broadhurst & Martin, 2014a
70. Bass, 2002; Wiggins, 1992, 2014
71. Cooper et al., 2017; Edwards, 1969, 1973, 1980; Wiggins, 1992, 2000; Wiggins & Miller, 2003
72. Babb, 2017; Branch, 2017; Brewer, 2017; Cooper et al., 2017; Edwards, 1969, 1973, 1980; Rogers, 2012
73. Rogers, 2012
74. Rogers, 2012
75. Cooper et al., 2017; Edwards, 1980; Rogers, 2012
76. Nathan, 2015; New, 2016; Terlep & Belkin, 2015; Tracy & Southall, 2015
77. Nathan, 2015; New, 2016; Terlep & Belkin, 2015; Tracy & Southall, 2015
78. Brewer, 2017; Cooper et al., 2017
79. Babb, 2017; Branch, 2017; Brewer, 2017; Edwards, 1969, 1973, 1980
80. King, 1968
81. Freire, 1970
82. Cooper et al., 2017, p. 11
83. Babb, 2017; Brewer, 2017; Cooper et al., 2017
84. Bailard, 2012
85. Duncan, 2018; Edwards, 1969, 1973, 1980; Rogers, 2012
86. Duncan, 2018
87. Rogers, 2012
88. Anderson, 2015; Rhoads, 1998
89. Anderson, 2015; George-Williams, 2019; Rhoads, 1998; Rogers, 2012; Washington, 2014
90. Broadhurst & Martin, 2014b; Rhoads, 1998, 2016; Rogers, 2012
91. Rogers, 2012, p. 71
92. Pew Research Center, 2017
93. Coates, 2015; Ferner & Wing, 2016; Tatum, 2017
94. Coates, 2015; Ferner & Wing, 2016; Tatum, 2017; West, 2017
95. Coates, 2015, p. 9
96. Coates, 2015, p. 78
97. Coates, 2015; Ferner & Wing, 2016; Tatum, 2017; West, 2017
98. Walsh, 1981; Washington, 2017
99. Jennings, 1999
100. Birkland 1998; Goss, 2001
101. Jasper & Poulsen, 1995
102. Morris & Braine, 2001
103. Coates, 2015; Nathan, 2015; New, 2016; Terlep & Belkin, 2015; Tracy & Southall, 2015; West, 2017
104. BLM, 2018
105. Chenoweth & Stephan, 2011; Ganz, 2006; Tilly, 2004
106. Keck & Sikkink, 1998
107. Rogers, 2012
108. Rhoads, 1998
109. CADSA, 2020
110. Joyce, 2014; Little, 2013
111. Vargas, 2008
112. Vargas, 2008, p. 26
113. Martin, 2005; Martin, Harrison, & Bukstein, 2010
114. Riffer, 1972

115. Assibey & Mensah, 1997
116. Yosso, 2005
117. Garza, 2017
118. Joseph, 2006a, 2006b; London & Warren, 2018; Rogers, 2012
119. Joseph, 2006a, 2006b; London & Warren, 2018; Rhoads, 1998; Rogers, 2012
120. Joseph, 2006a, 2006b; London & Warren, 2018; Rogers, 2012
121. Bauer, 1998, p. 2
122. Kuh & Whitt, 1998
123. Stolzenberg et al., 2020
124. Harper et al., 2011
125. Smith, 2004
126. Gorski, 2018a
127. Gorski, 2018b
128. Pines, 1994, p. 381
129. Asa, 2009
130. Dubois, 1903/1969, p. 45
131. Nolan, 2020
132. Garofoli, 2020
133. Branch, 2017
134. Cooper et al, 2017, p. 8; Rogers, 2012
135. Wiggins, 1992
136. Branch, 2017; Cooper et al., 2017; Edwards, 2016; George-Williams, 2019
137. George-Williams, 2019
138. Cooper, Macaulay, & Rodriguez, 2017; Edwards, 1969, 1980; Rogers, 2012; Wiggins, 2000
139. George-Williams, 2019
140. Nathan, 2015
141. Nathan, 2015
142. George-Williams, 2019
143. Bauer-Wolf, 2017; Dellenger, 2017; Spain, 2017
144. Stirgus, 2017, 2018
145. Nelson, 2017
146. Delgado & Stefancic, 2012; Ladson-Billings & Tate, 1995; Lynn & Dixson, 2013
147. Collins, 1986, 1990, 1991, 2000
148. Taylor, 1998
149. Collins, 2000, p. 25
150. Collins, 1990b; Taylor, 1998
151. Collins, 2000
152. Crenshaw, 2018
153. Collins, 1990b, 2000; Taylor, 1998b
154. Smith, 2010
155. Cooper et al., 2017
156. Quaye, Griffin, & Museus, 2015, p. 22
157. Museus, Ravello, & Vega, 2012
158. Biddix, 2014; Broadhurst & Martin, 2014a; Chambers & Phelps, 1993
159. Lorde, 1977

REFERENCES

Anderson, M. (2015). The other student activists. *The Atlantic.* https://www.theatlantic.com/education/archive/2015/11/student-activism-history-injustice/417129

Asa, R. (2009). Compassion fatigue: When caring hurts too much. *AGD Impact.* http://www.compassionfatigue.org/pages/agd.pdf

Ash, A. N. (2018). *The ecology of White anti-racism: Administrators and racial justice in Christian higher education* (UMI No. ED587782) [Doctoral dissertation]. ProQuest Dissertations and Theses database.

Aspen Initiative (2020). https://www.aspeninstitute.org/

Assibey-Mensah, G. O. (1997). Role models and youth development: Evidence and lessons from the perceptions of African-American male youth. *Western Journal of Black Studies, 21,* 242–251

Babb, K. (2017, August). The making of Colin Kaepernick. *Washington Post.* https://www.washingtonpost.com/sports/the-making-of-colin-kaepernick/2017/09/07/d4d58e20-9320-11e7-8754-d478688d23b4_story.html

Bahadur, N. (2020, August 23). *What no one tells Black women about breastfeeding.* Zora Medium. https://zora.medium.com/what-no-one-tells-black-women-about-breastfeeding-9d1c8af4bb08

Bailard, C. S. (2012). A field experiment on the Internet's effect in an African election: Savvier citizens, disaffected voters, or both? *Journal of Communication, 62,* 330–344.

Baker, A. (2007, March 17). 3 detectives are indicted in 50-shot killing in Queens. *New York Times.* https://www.nytimes.com/2007/03/17/nyregion/17grand.html

Bass, A. (2002). *Not the triumph but the struggle: The 1968 Olympics and the making of the Black athlete.* Minneapolis, MN: University of Minnesota Press.

Bauer, K. (1998). Campus climate: Understanding the critical components of today's colleges and universities. *New Directions for Institutional Research, 98,* 1–5

Bauer-Wolf, J. (2017, October). Free speech advocate silenced. *Inside Higher Education.* https://www.insidehighered.com/news/2017/10/06/william-mary-students-who-shut-down-aclu-event-broke-conduct-code

Biddix, J. P. (2014). Development through dissent: Campus activism as civic learning. *New Directions for Higher Education, 167,* 73–85.

Biondi, M. (2012). *Black revolution on campus.* Berkeley, CA: University of California Press. http://www.jstor.org/stable/10.1525/j.ctt1ppfmn

Birkland, T. A. (1998). Focusing events, mobilization, and agenda setting. *Journal of Public Policy, 18,* 53–75.

Black Lives Matter. (2018). https://blacklivesmatter.com

Bradley, S. M. (2016, February 1). Black activism on campus: A timeline. *New York Times.* https://www.nytimes.com/interactive/2016/02/07/education/edlife/Black-History-Activism-on-Campus-Timeline.html

Branch, J. (2017, September 7). The awakening of Colin Kaepernick. *New York Times.* https://www.nytimes.com/2017/09/07/sports/colin-kaepernick-nfl-protests.html

Brewer, J. (2017). Sorry for the inconvenience fans, but Black athlete activism is multiplying. *Washington Post.* https://www.washingtonpost.com/sports/sorry-for-the-inconvenience-fans-but-black-athlete-activism-is-multiplying/2017/08/16/ff2eb762-82a1-11e7-ab27-1a21a8e006ab_story.html

Broadhurst, C., & Martin, G. L. (2014b). Part of the "establishment"? Fostering positive campus climates for student activists. *Journal of College and Character, 15*(2), 75–86.

Broadhurst, C., & Martin, G. L. (Eds.). (2014a). Radical academia?: Understanding the climates for campus activists. In *New Directions for Higher Education* (pp. 31–41). San Francisco, CA: Jossey-Bass.

Centers for Disease Control and Prevention. (2020). https://www.cdc.gov/media/releases/2020/archives.html

Chambers, T., & Phelps, C. E. (1993). Student activism as a form of leadership and student development. *NASPA Journal, 31*(1), 19–29.

Chenoweth, E., & Stephan, M. (2011). *Why civil resistance works: The strategic logic of nonviolent conflict.* New York, NY: Columbia University Press.

Coalition for African Diaspora Student-Athletes. (CADSA, 2020). https://www.cadsanational.org

Coates, T. (2015). *Between the world and me.* New York, NY: Penguin Random House.

Collins, P. H. (1986). Learning from the outsider within: The sociological significance of Black feminist thought. *Social Problems, 33*(6), S14–S32.

Collins, P. H. (1990, 2000). *Black feminist thought: Knowledge, consciousness, and the politics of empowerment.* New York, NY: Routledge.

Collins, P. H. (1990b). *Towards an Afrocentric feminist epistemology.* London: Routledge.

Collins, S. C., & Jun, A. (2017). *White out: Understanding White privilege and dominance in the modern age.* New York, NY: Peter Lang.

Cooper, J. N., Macaulay, C., & Rodriguez, S. H. (2017). Race and resistance: A typology of African American sport activism. *International Review for the Sociology of Sport, 52,* 1–31.

Crenshaw, K. (1989). Demarginalizing the intersection of race and sex: A Black feminist critique of antidiscrimination doctrine, feminist theory and antiracist politics. *University of Chicago Legal Forum, 8.*

Crenshaw, K. (1991). Mapping the margins: Intersectionality, identity politics, and violence against women of color. *Stanford Law Review, 43,* 1241–1299.

Crenshaw, K. (1995). The identity factor in multiculturalism. *Liberal Education, 81*(4), 6–11.

Crenshaw, K. (2018, April 2). *Her dream deferred: A week on the status of Black women and girls series.* African American Policy Forum (AAPF). A Dream Deferred Conference. https://www.essence.com/news/dream-deferred-conference-black-women

Cromer, C. & Millan, A. (2020). Resources to Combat Structural Racism in America. Aspen Institute. https://www.aspeninstitute.org/blog-posts/resources-to-combat-structural-racism-in-america/

Dancy, T. E., Edwards, K. T., & Davis, J. (2018, February). Historically White universities and plantation politics: Anti-Blackness and higher education in the Black Lives Matter era. *Urban Education, 53,* 176–195.

Delgado, R., & Stefancic, J. (2012). *Critical race theory: An introduction.* New York, NY: NYU Press.

Dubois, W. E. B. (1903,1969). *The souls of Black folks.* Chicago, IL: McClurg.

Dumas, M. J. (2010). What is this 'Black' in Black education? Imagining a cultural politics without guarantees. In Z. Leonardo (Ed.), *Handbook of cultural politics and education* (pp. 403–422). Boston, MA: Sense Publishers.

Dumas, M. J. (2015). Contesting White accumulation: Toward a materialist anti-racist analysis of school desegregation. In K. Bowman (Ed.), *The pursuit of racial and ethnic equality in American public schools: Mendez, Brown, and beyond* (pp. 291–311). Lansing, MI: Michigan State University Press.

Dumas, M. J. (2016). Against the dark: Antiblackness in education policy and discourse. *Theory Into Practice, 55,* 11–19.

Duncan, G. A. (2018). *Black Panther Party: American organization.* Britannica. https://www.britannica.com/topic/Black-Panther-Party

Eagan, K., Stolzenberg, E. B., Bates, A. K., Aragon, M. C., Suchard, M. R., & Rios-Aguilar, C. (2015). *The American freshman: National norms fall 2015.* Los Angeles, CA: Higher Education Research Institute, UCLA.

Edwards, H. (1969). *The revolt of the Black athlete.* New York, NY: Free Press.

Edwards, H. (1973). *Sociology of sport.* Homewood, IL: Dorsey Press.

Edwards, H. (1980). *The struggle that must be: An autobiography.* New York, NY: MacMillan.

Ellis, C. (2004). *The ethnographic I.* Walnut Creek, CA: AltaMira.

Feagin, J. R. (2001). Social justice and sociology: Agendas for the twenty-first century: Presidential address. *American Sociological Review, 66*(1), 1–20.

Ferner, N., & Wing, M. (2016). This was one of the safest years ever for police, so let's put that 'war on cops' thing to rest. *Huffington Post.* https://www.huffpost.com/entry/2015-safest-years-war-oncops_n_567b0d83e4b0b958f6592cff

Flowers, S. H. (1998). Coming of age under protest: African American college students in the 1960s. In G. J. DeGroot (Ed.), *Student protest: The sixties and after* (pp. 169–185). New York, NY: Addison Wesley Longman.

Freire, P. (1970). *Pedagogy of the oppressed.* New York, NY: Continuum.

Ganz, M. (2006). *Organizing: People, power and change.* Cambridge, MA: Harvard Kennedy School of Government.

Garofoli, J. (2020, June 8). Being a white ally of African Americans means more than just protesting. *San Francisco Chronicle.* https://www.sfchronicle.com/politics/article/Being-a-white-ally-of-African-Americans-means-15321365.php

Garza, A. (2017, February 1). *Behind the hashtag #BlackLivesMatter.* Lecture presented at the University of California, Riverside, CA

George-Williams, G. (2019). *Love is at the root of resistance: A hermeneutic phenomenological inquiry into the lived experiences of Black college athlete activists.* (Order No. 13898234) [Doctoral dissertation, Azusa Pacific University]. ProQuest Publishing.

Gorski, P. (2018a). Fighting racism, battling burnout: Causes of activist burnout in US racial justice activists. *Ethnic and Racial Studies, 42,* 667–687.

Gorski, P. (2018b). Racial battle fatigue and activist burnout in racial justice activists of color at predominantly white colleges and universities. *Race, Ethnicity, and Education.* https://doi.org/10.1080/13613324.2018.1497966

Goss, K. A. (2001). *The smoking gun: How focusing events transform politics.* Cambridge, MA: Harvard Kennedy School of Government.

Harper, S. R. (2012a). *Black male student success in higher education: A report from the National Black Male College Achievement Study.* Philadelphia, PA: University of Pennsylvania, Center for the Study of Race and Equity in Education.

Harper, S. R., & Hurtado, S. (Eds.). (2011). *Racial and ethnic diversity in higher education* (3rd ed.). Boston, MA: Pearson.

hooks, b. (2013). *Writing beyond race: Living theory and practice.* New York, NY: Routledge.

Hulme, E. (2018). Personal communication (January 7, 2018). Azusa Pacific University.

Jasper, J. M., & Poulsen, J. (1995). Recruiting strangers and friends: Moral shocks and social networks in animal rights and anti-nuclear protests. *Social Problems, 42,* 493–512.

Jennings, M. K. (1999). Political responses to pain and loss. *The American Political Science Review, 93,* 1–13.

Joseph, P. E. (2006a*). Waiting 'til the midnight hour: A narrative history of Black Power in America.* New York, NY: Henry Holt and Co.

Joseph, P. E. (Ed.). (2006b). *The Black Power movement.* New York, NY: Routledge.

Joyce, M. (2014). *Activism success: A concept explication* [Unpublished master's thesis]. University of Washington, Seattle, WA.

Keck, M. E., & Sikkink, K. (1998). *Activists beyond borders: Advocacy networks in international politics.* Ithaca, NY: Cornell University Press.

Kuh, G. D., & Whitt, E. J. (1998).The invisible tapestry: Culture in American colleges and universities. *ASHE-ERIC Higher Education Report,* 1.

Ladson-Billings, G. J., & Tate, W. F. (1995). Toward a critical race theory of education. *Teachers College Record, 97,* 47–68.

Lee, W. (2015). *Moving toward social justice in sport: A comprehensive study of social justice activists in sport and the factors that shape them.* (Order No. 155205) [Doctoral dissertation]. ProQuest Dissertations and Theses database.

Lindsay-Dennis, L. (2015). Black feminist-womanist research paradigm: Toward a culturally relevant research model focused on African American girls. *Journal of Black Studies, 46*(5), 506–520.

Little, W. (2013). *Introduction to sociology.* Rice University. OpenStax College. Creative Commons Attribution 3.0 Unported License. https://my.uopeople.edu/pluginfile.php/57436/mod_book/chapter/37634/SOC1502.Textbook.pdf

Loewy, T. (2014, December 4). *Knox College basketball player Ariyana Smith says protest 'last resort.'* https://www.galesburg.com/article/20141204/news/141209906

London, E., & Warren, L. Y. (2018). *The intersection of youth activism and faith-based values.* Center for American Progress. https://www.americanprogress.org/issues/religion/news/2018/04/06/449150/inters ection-youth-activism-faith-based-values

Lorde, A. G. (1977). *Your silence will not protect your speech.* [Video]. YouTube. https://www.youtube.com/watch?v=K0MHGR1VYjE

Lynn, M., & Dixson, A. D. (Eds.). (2013). *Handbook of critical race theory in education.* New York, NY: Routledge.

Martin, B. E. (2005). *A phenomenological study of academically driven African American male student-athletes at highly selective universities* [Unpublished doctoral dissertation]. University of Southern California, Los Angeles, CA.

Martin, B., Harrison, C. K., & Bukstein, S. (2010). "It takes a village" for African American male scholar-athletes. *Journal for the Study of Sports and Athletes in Education, 4,* 277–295.

Maslow, A. H. (1943). A theory of human motivation. *Psychological Review, 50*(4), 370–396.

Millennial Impact Report (MIR). (2017). *Year in review: An invigorated generation for causes and social issues.* http://www.themillennialimpact.com/past-research

Mills, C. W. (1997). *The racial contract.* Ithaca: NY: Cornell University Press.

Moeschberger, S. L., Ordonez, A., Shankar, J., & Raney, S. (2006). Moving from contact to change. In R. L. Toporek et al. (Eds.), *Handbook for social justice in counseling psychology: Leadership, vision, and action* (pp. 472–486). Thousand Oaks, CA: SAGE.

Morris, A. D., & Braine, N. (2001). Social movements and oppositional consciousness. In J. Mansbridge & A. Morris (Eds.), *Oppositional consciousness: The subjective roots of social protest* (pp. 20–37). Chicago, IL: University of Chicago Press.

Museus, S. D., Ravello, J. N., & Vega, B. E. (2012). The campus racial culture: A critical race counterstory. In S. D. Museus & U. M. Jayakumar (Eds.), *Creating campus cultures: Fostering success among racially diverse student populations* (pp. 106–129). New York, NY: Routledge.

Nathan, A. (2015). Tim Wolfe resigns as Missouri president after boycott by football team. *Bleacher Report.* https://bleacherreport.com/articles/2587163-black-missouri-football-players-boycotting-until-school-president-resigns

Nelson, K. (2017). The importance of student leadership. About Leaders. https://aboutleaders.com/student-leadership/#gs.7xazuc

New, J. (2016). Get ready for more protests. *Inside Higher Ed.* https://www.insidehighered.com/news/2016/02/11/survey-finds-nearly-1-10freshmen-plan-participating-campus-protests

Nolan, E. (2020). '13th' Netflix documentary viewers surge by 4,665 percent in three weeks. *Newsweek.* https://www.newsweek.com/13th-netflix-youtube-documentary-watch-ava-duvernay-race-movies-1511535

Padesky, C. A. & Mooney, K. A. (2012). Strengths-based cognitive-behavioural therapy: A four-step model to build resilience. *Clinical Psychology and Psychotherapy, 19,* 283–290.

Patton, L. D.; McEwen, M; Rendón, L; Howard-Hamilton, M. F. (2007). Critical Race Perspectives on Theory in Student Affairs. *New Directions for Student Services, 120,* 39–53.

Pew Research Center U.S. Politics and Policy. (2017, December 19). *Most Americans say Trump's election has led to worse race relations in the U.S.* http://www.people-press.org/2017/12/19/most-americans-say-trumps-election-has-led-to-worse-race-relations-in-the-u-s

Pines, A. (1994). Burnout in political activism: An existential perspective. *Journal of Health and Human Resources Administration, 164,* 381–394.

Quaye, S. J., Griffin, K. A., & Museus, S. D. (2015). Engaging students of color. In S. J. Quaye & S. R. Harper (Eds.), *Student engagement in higher education: Theoretical perspectives and practical approaches for diverse populations* (2nd ed., pp. 21–48). New York, NY: Routledge.

Racial Equity Tools. (2020). https://www.racialequitytools.org

Rhoads, R. A. (1998). *Freedom's web: Student activism in an age of cultural diversity.* Baltimore, MD: Johns Hopkins University Press.

Riffer, R. L. (1972). Determinants of university students' political attitudes or demythologizing campus political activism. *Review of Educational Research, 42,* 561–571.

Rogers, I. H. (2012). The Black campus movement and the institutionalization of Black studies, 1965–1970. *Journal of African American Studies, 16*(1), 21–40.

Rye, A. (2017, February 24). Angela Rye: I always knew I was Black. *CNN Opinion.* https://www.cnn.com/2017/02/24/opinions/always-knew-my-blackness-rye-opinion

Sampson, E. E., & Korn, H. A. (1970). *Student activism and protest.* San Francisco, CA: Jossey-Bass.

Shaw, R. (1990). *The activist's handbook: A primer for the 1990s and beyond.* Berkeley, CA: University of California Press.

Smith, W. A. (2004). Black faculty coping with racial battle fatigue: The campus racial climate in a post-civil rights era. In D. Cleveland (Ed.), *A long way to go: Conversations about race by African American faculty and graduate students* (pp. 171–190). New York, NY: Peter Lang.

Smith, W. A. (2010). Toward an understanding of Black misandric microaggressions and racial battle fatigue in historically White institutions. In V. C. Polite (Ed.), *The state of the African American male in Michigan: A courageous conversation* (pp. 265–277). East Lansing, MI: Michigan State University Press.

Solorzano, D. G., Allen, W., & Carroll, G. (2002). Keeping race in place: Racial microaggressions and campus racial climate at the University of California, Berkeley. *Chicana/o Latina/o Law Review, 23*(1) 15–111.

Spain, K. (2017). LSU sends email to athletes about expressing opinions on Alton Sterling case. *USA Today Sports.* https://www.usatoday.com/story/sports/ncaaf/sec/2017/05/03/lsu-tigers-student-athletes-expressing-opinions-alton-sterling-case/101261634

Stirgus, E. (2017, October 17). KSU change won't stop their kneeling protest, cheerleaders say. *Atlanta Journal-Constitution.* https://www.ajc.com/news/local-education/ksu-didn-follow-guidance-cheerleader-kneeling/CDKOAKt4idekbBTeoodTwJ

Stirgus, E. (2018). 4 of 5 KSU cheerleaders in anthem protest say they weren't picked for this year's squad. https://www.wsbtv.com/news/local/cobbcounty/4-or-5-ksu-cheerleaders-in-anthem-protest-say-they-weren-t-picked-forthis-year-s-squad/818409548

Stolzenberg, B., Aragon, M. C., Romo, E., Couch, V., McLennan, D., Eagan, M. K., & Kang, N. (2020). *The American freshman: National norms, Fall 2019.* Higher Education Research Institute, UCLA.

Tait, L. T., Jr., & Van Gorder, C. (2002). *Three-fifths theology: Challenging racism in American Christianity.* Trenton, NJ: Africa World Press.

Tatum, B. (1997; 2017). *Why are all the Black kids sitting together in the cafeteria?: And other conversations about race.* New York, NY: Basic Books.

Taylor, D., & Clark, M. P. (2009). Set up to fail: Institutional racism and the sabotage of school improvement. *Equity & Excellence in Education, 42*(2), 114–129.

Taylor, U. (1998). The historical evolution of Black feminist theory and praxis. *Journal of Black Studies, 29,* 234–253.

Terlep, S., & Belkin, D. (2015, November 8). Mizzou athletic department backs Black football players on boycott. *The Wall Street Journal.* https://www.wsj.com/articles/minority-players-on-university-of-missouri-football-team-threaten-boycott-1446997013

Tilly, C. (2004). *Social movements, 1768–2004.* Boulder, CO: Paradigm.

Tracy, M., & Southall, A. (2015, November 8). Black football players lend heft to protests at Missouri. *New York Times.* https://www.nytimes.com/2015/11/09/us/missouri-football-players-boycott-in-protest-of-university-president.html

Vargas, R. (2008). *Family activism: Empowering your community, beginning with family and friends.* San Francisco, CA: Berrett-Koehler.

Walsh, E. J. (1981). Resource mobilization and citizen protest in communities around Three Mile Island. *Social Problems, 29*(1), 1–21. https://doi.org/10.2307/800074

Washington, J. (2017, January 4). Winning isn't the only thing: Caring for Black student-athletes: Summit examines issues of race in high-level college sports. *The Undefeated.* https://theundefeated.com/features/black-student-athlete-summit-at-university-of-texas-focuses-on-racial-issues

West, C. (2017, February 24). *Justice matters.* [Presentation] Pepperdine University, Malibu, CA.

Wiggins, D. K. (1992). "The year of the awakening": Black athletes, racial unrest, and the Civil Rights Movement of 1968. *The International Journal of the History of Sport, 9,* 188–208.

Wiggins, D. K. (2000). Critical events affecting racism in athletics. In D. Brooks & R. Althouse (Eds.), *Racism in college athletics: The African American athlete's experience* (2nd ed., pp. 15–36). Morgantown, WV: Fitness Information Technology.

Wiggins, D. K. (2014). "The struggle that must be": Harry Edwards, sport, and the fight for racial equality. *The International Journal of the History of Sport, 31,* 760–777.

Wiggins, D. K., & Miller, P. (2003). *The unlevel playing field: A documentary history of the African-American experience in sport.* Urbana, IL: University of Illinois Press.

Yosso, T. J. (2005). Whose culture has capital? *Race, Ethnicity, and Education, 8*(1), 6991.

ACKNOWLEDGMENTS

How dare I write a book and not honor and acknowledge the people and places that have molded, motivated, and raised me. I am indebted to you.

People

To my family—both those who do and do not share DNA with me. Words cannot describe my gratitude and love. To the women who have raised me, Gerri George, Nauty Red, and Kim. You three have taught me to love without ceasing, love the word of God, and be brave in the face of adversity and turmoil.

To my brothers, Gerrence and Gyade, who never allow me to take myself too seriously and have held very necessary roast fests since Day One that made my skin thick! I will always remember our latchkey kid moments and watching *Twilight Zone* marathons. You two are my originators of Black boy joy. I love you two so much.

To the OGs in my life! The women who have been in my life for more than 25 years: Josephine, Rhonda, Lindsey, Myesha, Erika, and Heather. I'm talking bangs with an ungodly amount of hairspray, the Merkur Scorpio, our love for Tupac, the Jetta, dancing the night away at Status, piling into the Honda Civic, and all the '90s R & B (to this day). You knew me before I knew myself. We are now wives, mamas, badass bosses and entrepreneurs, and I thank you for never changing your core.

To my Ph.D. dolls, Joan Chittister once said, "Friendships with women are not just a social act. It's a spiritual act." CG, Cibele, Gina, Marjorie, Monica, and Kathy. My life will never be the same, and it is because of you six beautiful souls. We are walking through life together, and because of this truth, I have gained six sisters for life. May the Lord continue to light our paths to righteousness. Thank you for being my cheerleaders and hype squad.

To the village of surrogate mamas in my life. You may not have birthed me, but you loved, embraced, and kept me accountable like I was your own. You are appreciated beyond measure.

To the entire faculty and staff in the doctoral program in higher education at Azusa Pacific University. I am so grateful for your love and support during my doctoral journey. I became a scholar activist under your care.

Dr. Laurie Schreiner, thank you for your leadership as chair of the higher education department; you are an example of what a dynamic change leader looks like. We always know you have our best interests and will advocate for us. I am forever grateful for you.

Dr. Alexander Jun, you were the perfect head coach for this athlete during my dissertation and I value your continuous support. You knew when to challenge me to improve my game and when to trust me to slow my shot down and perfect my dissertation.

Dr. Tabatha Jones Jolivet, my dissertation doula. Your spirit, guidance, and unapologetic love for our community allowed me space to birth work of which I am continuously and profoundly proud.

To my activist ancestors both past and present (you were, so that I can be):

- James Baldwin

- Black Lives Matter, the founders and all who have committed to the fight for liberation

- Black Panther Party for Self-Defense

- Angela Davis

- Fred Hampton

- Colin Kaepernick

- Audre Geraldine Lorde

- National Women's Basketball Association

- Huey P. Newton

- Malcolm X

And so many more.

To the Black Doctoral Student Association at Azusa Pacific University and the first e-board. Thank you for trusting my vision to create a legacy for all Black doctoral students to come. To the current members of the Black Doctoral Student Association, keep pushing and never give up. Continue the legacy and shine, Black scholars.

What would this book be without guidance, support, and, most important, edits and revisions? Absolutely nothing. To Sedrik and Linda. I have deep gratitude for your lens and direction through this book. Don't you just love divine connections? Thank you for being a part of creating this magic. I can't wait for the next adventure!

Places

I am a product of the South and the Great Migration. To New Orleans, LA, Mama's hometown; and Alabama, my daddy's place of birth; and California where I was born and raised. The beautiful blend of the richness of the South and the diverse tapestry that is California. I am because of such marriage.

I want to center a little community within a city, Phillips Ranch! Born and raised there the first 25 years of my life, I will never forget the block parties, Daddy BBQing, music blasting, Mama and Daddy dancing until late at night, and all our neighbors who opened their houses to us. A moment in time where true community and diversity thrived. I am so blessed to have been raised in such a place.

To the schools and places that contributed to the pieces of me. My places of learning and unlearning, which I will cherish forever:

- Lorbeer Middle School

- Diamond Bar High School

- Mt. San Antonio College

- California State University, Los Angeles

- University of La Verne

- Azusa Pacific University

To all those I may have forgotten to include, please know that every conversation and interaction we have had has contributed to this moment in my life.

ABOUT THE AUTHOR

Gyasmine George-Williams, Ph.D., also known as "Dr. G," is an activist, credentialed socio-cultural practitioner, and professor. She earned her bachelor's degree in Psychology from CSU Los Angeles and a master's degree in College Counseling and Student Services as well as a master's in Educational Counseling with a Pupil Personnel Services Credential from the University of La Verne. She earned her Ph.D. in Higher Education from Azusa Pacific University.

In addition to her academic background, she is the child of activists. Her father was a former member of the Black Panther Party for Self-Defense, and her mother served as an educational activist and as a teacher in the Los Angeles Unified School District for 37 years. Dr. G's research and passion includes student activism, the interaction between students of color and faculty, women of color in leadership, and critical race theory in higher education. She is a frequent presenter at conferences throughout North America and internationally, including the National Conference on Race and Ethnicity in American Higher Education (NCORE), the Black Student Athlete Summit, the International Activism Conference, the Advancing Women in Leadership Conference, and at the University of the Western Cape in South Africa.

Dr. G has created research-based models curated to honor and center the experiences of activists. The Activism Growth Model™ is a guide for student activists in this very timely moment on how to utilize their voices for change. The Black Athlete Activist Leadership Model™ is designed to enable stakeholders (including coaches, administrators, and institutions) to serve athlete activists and activists of color holistically. She is also the founder of GGW Consulting, consulting rooted in advocacy.